MORE FAST & FANTASTIC

A WONDERFUL COLLECTION OF LIGHTER, QUICK TO PREPARE RECIPES

A fund raising project for
non-profit associations

The cover photo taken and donated by
Derik Murray Photography Inc.

Copyright © 1990 by North Shore Family Services Society
1st Printing October, 1990

Canadian Cataloguing in Publication Data

Main entry under title:

More fast & fantastic

Includes index.
ISBN 0-9694116-1-8

1. Quick and easy cookery. I. North Shore Family
Services Society. II. Title: More fast and
fantastic.
TX833.5.M67 1990 641.5'55 C90-091713-X

Designer Karole Doner
Illustrator Valerie Berry
Typeset by Hilary Powell
Cover colour separations donated by Total Graphics,
Vancouver
Cover design by McKim Advertising, Vancouver
Printed in Canada by D.W. Friesen & Son Ltd.

More Fast and Fantastic was produced by a group of volunteers as a fund raising project for the North Shore Family Services Society. They also brought you *Fast and Fantastic*, which became a Canadian Best Seller and sold over 16,000 copies. The recipes in this new cookbook have an emphasis on lighter cooking and healthier foods for the new decade. Recipes marked with ♡ have been analyzed by the School of Family and Nutritional Sciences at the University of British Columbia. These recipes meet the fat and salt criteria of the Heart and Stroke Foundation of Canada's Heart Smart Restaurant Program. The recipe analyses for this book were paid for by the Heart and Stroke Foundation of BC and Yukon in the interest of promoting healthy food choices.

The North Shore Family Services Society is a multi-service, nonprofit agency dedicated, through a wide variety of programs and services, to enriching and strengthening family life in British Columbia. The agency has made this new cookbook available to other nonprofit organizations for their own fund raising projects. By buying this cookbook you have made an important contribution to valuable community work.

Thank you.

On behalf of the North Shore Family Services Society, board, staff and clients, we wish to extend our thanks to all those individuals who have contributed to the production of our second cookbook.

When our first book *Fast and Fantastic* attained best seller status, we decided to try for a repeat performance, this time presenting recipes with a lighter theme in keeping with the healthier eating habits of the 1990's.

Once again, we are so grateful to the recipe testers, the artists and the proofreaders. We are especially indebted to our loving and patient friends and families who joined us in the critical analysis of all these recipes.

As a result of your labours, all proceeds from the sale of this book will help to finance the many programs offered by North Shore Family Services and other community agencies.

We wish to acknowledge the following individuals:

Sue Bauman   John Burrowes   Ginny Crawford   Arlene Gladstone
Gary Grafton   Ken Hanna   Valerie Houck   Pat Kayll   Carlota Lee
Gail Marus   Barb Moi   Pat Orr   Ida Paddock   Cathie Sabiston
Sharon Shorter   Peter Speck
Simon Fraser University Small Business Counselling Group
Faculty of Business Administration

The Cookbook Committee:

Doreen Ramage, Chairman
Diane Whyte
Jill Flemons

We gratefully acknowledge our contributors who so enthusiastically shared with us their new or treasured recipes:

Joan Akers
Ann Ashcroft
Lorna Baker
Joan Barter
Sue Bauman
Betty Beaton
Jessie Begbie
Betty Begg
Valerie Berry
Joyce Birch
Li Boesen
Brenda Bond
Barbara Bosdet
Lara Bosdet
Yvonne Bower
Sylvia Brewster
Ruth Brock
Joan Brown
Dorothy Brown
Shirley Butterworth
Nicola Cavendish
Wendy Chandler
Eileen Crawford
Ginny Crawford
Lee Crawford
Muriel Croft
Roger Dancey
Mary Ellen de Grace
Janet de Savoye
Catherine Devins
Bonnie Dodd
David Dustan
Yulanda Faris
Dorothy Findlay
Jill Flemons
Patricia Fraser
Pat Garven
Wilma Gibson
Arlene Gladstone
Jurgen Gothe
Barbara Grais
Betty Green

Irene Grinke
Elio Guarnori
Joan Hamanishi
Sigrun Hanna
Mary Hill
Kathy Hogarth
Johanne Homer
Michel Jacob
Maxine Johnson
Pat Kayll
Sharon Kennedy
Fanny Kiefer
Rose Mary Lang
Vera Lees
Carrie Lehman
Judy Langstaff
Otto Lowy
Anna Luckyj
Ann McBride
May MacDonald
Connie McGill
Joan McKone
Linda McKone
Georgie McLeod
Barbara McQuade
David McSherry
Wendy McSorley
Diane Markey
Suzanne Marks
Brenda Martin
Miriam Martin
Gail Marus
Caroline Mason
Barbara Meistrich
Christine Miller
Karen Milos
Barb Moi
Ann Mortifee
Dorthy Munroe
Tazeem Nathoo
Charlotte Nelson
Patricia Newcombe

Katherine Newman
Ida Paddock
Barbara Pierce
M Radford
Myrtle Ramage
Doreen Ramage
Elise Rees
Sheila Reid
Barb Reid
Dianne Rice
Carol Ritter
Marilyn Ross
Cathie Sabiston
Victoria Scudamore
Cathy Sheehan
Kayla Shoctor
Loretta Sieben
Annie Smith
Alison Solven
Glenda Solven
Dodie Thompson
LaVerne Thompson
Judy Thorson
Linda Tournier
Hazel Turner
Jo Vance
Sharon Westin
Mary White
Anne Whyte
Diana Whyte
Jean Wood

Cover Recipe

Poached prawns set on Sour Sweet Lime Coulis   **Page 54**
Cooked rice, pressed in oiled molds and unmolded
Steamed asparagus with pimiento strip
Garnish: lime twist and dill sprig

Recipes marked with ♡ meet the fat and salt criteria of the Heart
and Stroke Foundation of Canada's Heart Smart Restaurant Program.

Table of Contents

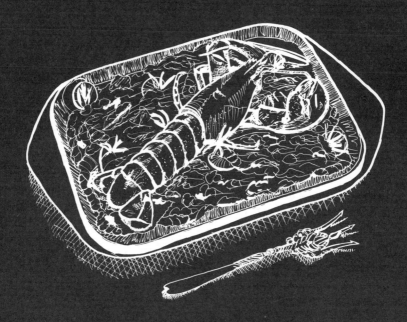

Hors d'oeuvres

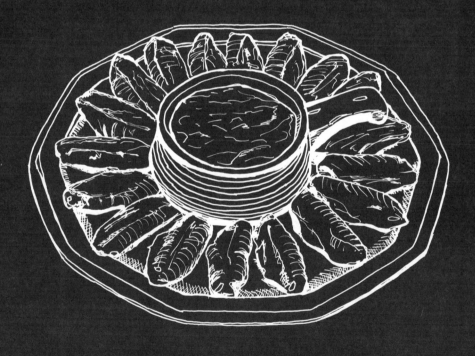

Curried Chicken Almond Rolls

Pull these out of the freezer when hungry guests arrive.

1	cup	finely chopped cooked chicken	250 mL
1	cup	mayonnaise	250 mL
¾	cup	shredded Monterey cheese	175 mL
⅓	cup	finely chopped almonds	75 mL
¼	cup	chopped fresh parsley	50 mL
2		large shallots, finely chopped	2
2	tsp	curry powder	10 mL
2	tsp	lemon juice	10 mL
½	tsp	pepper	2 mL
18		crustless slices whole wheat sandwich bread	18
¼	cup	melted butter	50 mL

Preheat oven to 375°F (190°C).
Combine the first 9 ingredients in a bowl, blending well. Cover and refrigerate for 30 minutes. Flatten bread slices with a rolling pin. Spread 1 Tbsp (15mL) of chicken mixture on each slice and roll up. Cut each roll in half and secure with a toothpick. Place on lightly greased baking sheet seam side down and brush with melted butter. Bake for 15 minutes. Remove toothpick before serving.
Note: These appetizers may be frozen after cooling. To reheat bake frozen rolls in 400°F (200°C) oven for 10 minutes or until hot.
Makes 36 appetizers.

Hot Tropical Wings

A new twist for an old favourite.

3	lb	chicken wings, cut at joints and tips discarded	1.5 kg
½	cup	tequila	125 mL
½	cup	chopped cilantro	125 mL
½	cup	lime or lemon marmalade	125 mL
3	Tbsp	fresh lemon juice	45 mL
2	Tbsp	olive oil	30 mL
1	tsp	Tabasco sauce	5 mL
1	tsp	grated lemon peel	5 mL
½	tsp	coarsely ground pepper	2 mL
3		cloves garlic, minced	3

Preheat oven to 350°F (180°C).
Place wing segments in a large flat dish or ziplock plastic bag. Combine remaining ingredients and pour over wings. Refrigerate 24 hours, turning pieces several times. Remove from marinade and place in a large shallow baking pan.
Bake for 30 minutes. While chicken bakes, pour marinade into a heavy saucepan and boil until reduced by half, stirring frequently. Preheat broiler and place chicken 6" (15cm) from heat. Baste with thickened sauce. Broil until crisp, turning and basting several times. Serves 8-10.

Mushroom Toast Cups

This make ahead appetizer is a crowd pleaser.

30		3" (7.5cm) rounds cut from thinly sliced bread butter for bread	30
¼	cup	butter	50 mL
¼	cup	chopped green onion	50 mL
1	lb	finely chopped mushrooms	500 g
3	Tbsp	flour	45 mL
1	cup	canned evaporated milk	250 mL
1	Tbsp	Dijon mustard	15 mL
1	Tbsp	chopped fresh parsley	15 mL
½	Tbsp	lemon juice	7 mL
⅛	tsp	cayenne pepper salt and pepper to taste paprika	.5 mL

Preheat oven to 350°F (180°C).
To prepare toast cups, butter both sides of bread rounds and fit into muffin cups.
Bake for 10 minutes. Cool on rack. Cups may be frozen at this point.
For filling, sauté onion in butter until tender. Add mushrooms, and cook gently. Stir in flour. Add milk, stirring until thickened. Add the next 6 ingredients. Filling may be refrigerated until needed. Place filling in toast cups and sprinkle with paprika.
Bake for 10 minutes or until hot. Serve immediately.
Makes 30 appetizers.

Hot Shrimp Pâté

A speciality of Fanny Kiefer who appears Monday nights on CBC TV's environment program, Down to Earth.

8	oz	cream cheese	250 g
2	Tbsp	mayonnaise	30 mL
1	tsp	curry, or more to taste	5 mL
		dash of Worcestershire sauce	
		chopped green onions	
½	lb	shrimp	250 g

Preheat oven to 375°F (190°C).
Whip cream cheese and mayonnaise, add the remaining ingredients.
Place in a small baking dish.
Bake for 15-20 minutes.
Serve with baguette, pumpernickel bread or crackers.
Note: Crab or a mixture of half shrimp, half crab may be substituted for the shrimp.
Serves a crowd.

Peppered Camembert Cheese

1	pkg Camembert cheese, split horizontally, cut side up	1
	red pepper jelly or green jalapeño pepper jelly	
	slivered almonds	

Spread jelly over each cheese half. Sprinkle almonds on top. Heat in microwave for 1½ minutes on full power or bake in 500°F (260°C) oven for 5 minutes. Serve with crackers.
Note: At Christmastime, try red jelly on one cheese half and green jelly on the other.
Serves a crowd.

Shrimp Muenster Roll

Your guests will love this appetizer.

1½	cups	shredded Muenster cheese	375 mL
1	cup	fresh shrimp, chopped	250 mL
¼	cup	thinly sliced green onions	50 mL
2		eggs	2
⅛	tsp	each salt, paprika, pepper and fresh dill, or to taste	.5 mL
1		pkg refrigerated crescent rolls	1
1	Tbsp	butter, melted	15 mL
1		egg yolk, beaten with	1
1	Tbsp	water	15 mL

Preheat oven to 400°F (200°C).
Combine the first 8 ingredients and set aside. Unroll crescent rolls, fold in half crosswise and roll out to a 14x9" (36x23cm) rectangle. Brush with butter. Spread shrimp mixture in 2" (5cm) strip along one long edge of dough. Roll up as for jelly roll, sealing seam and ends well. Carefully place roll onto ungreased cookie sheet. Brush with egg yolk water mixture.
Bake for 25 minutes or until golden brown.
Cool on rack 20 minutes. Cut into ½" (1cm) slices with a sharp knife.
Makes 28 appetizers.

Shrimp Temptations

A favourite appetizer with the soccer crowd!

1	lb	fresh shrimp	500 g
½	cup	finely chopped celery	125 mL
1½	Tbsp	mayonnaise	22 mL
½	tsp	onion powder	2 mL
¼	tsp	ground pepper	1 mL
1	loaf	cocktail rye bread	1
		butter	
		Thousand Island dressing	
		seafood cocktail sauce	
		dried sweet basil	

Combine the first 5 ingredients. Butter bread slices and spread with dressing. Mound shrimp onto bread as for an open-faced sandwich. Top each canapé with a dab of cocktail sauce and sprinkle with basil. Makes about 24 appetizers.

Big Hit Spinach Balls

Keep a stock in your freezer!

2		pkg (10oz/300g) frozen chopped spinach, drained and squeezed	2
2	cups	frozen herb stuffing	500 mL
1	cup	grated parmesan cheese	250 mL
¼	cup	melted butter	50 mL
4		green onions, chopped	4
3		eggs	3

Preheat oven to 350°F (180°C).
Combine all the ingredients and shape into small walnut size balls.
May be frozen at this point. Thaw slightly before baking.
Bake for 15 minutes. Serve with Dijon mustard for dipping.
Serves a crowd.

Hot Ham Fondue

1		round sourdough loaf	1
6	oz	cream cheese, softened	170 g
2	cups	grated cheddar cheese	500 mL
1	cup	finely diced ham	250 mL
1½	cups	light sour cream	375 mL
½	cup	chopped green onions	125 mL
1	tsp	Worcestershire sauce	5 mL

Preheat oven to 350°F (180°C).
Cut slice from top of bread and set aside. Remove bread from inside of loaf. Mix together the remaining ingredients and pack into the hollow loaf. Replace top slice. Wrap bread in foil.
Bake for 1½ hours.
Serve hot with raw veggies for dipping.
Serves 10-12.

Whispering Oyster Spread

1		pkg (8oz/250g) cream cheese, light or regular, softened	1
1		can (3.7oz/104g) smoked oysters, drained	1
¼	cup	light salad dressing	50 mL
3	Tbsp	lemon juice	45 mL
3	Tbsp	finely chopped pecans	45 mL
2	Tbsp	finely chopped onion	30 mL
¼	tsp	salt (optional)	1 mL
		freshly ground pepper	

In a blender or food processor combine the first 4 ingredients until smooth. Stir in the remaining ingredients. Cover and chill for several hours. Serve with assorted crackers.
Makes approximately 2 cups (500mL).

Marvelous Mussels

Serve with lots of crusty bread.

2	lb	fresh mussels, scrubbed and beards removed	1 kg
1		can (28oz/750mL) Italian spice stewed tomatoes	1
1		large onion, chopped	1
¾	cup	dry white wine	175 mL
¾	cup	tomato juice	175 mL
4		cloves garlic, minced	4
¼	cup	chopped green onions	50 mL
¼	tsp	oregano	1 mL
¼	tsp	thyme	1 mL
¼	tsp	pepper	1 mL
		celery seed and cayenne pepper to taste	

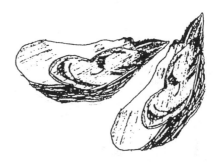

Place mussels in a bowl of cold water and soak for 1 hour. Combine the remaining ingredients in a large saucepan and bring to a boil. Cook for 3-4 minutes. Add mussels, cover the pan and cook over low heat for 5 minutes or until mussels open. Discard any that fail to open.

Serves 4-6 as an appetizer or 2 as an entrée.

Broccoli Brownies

2		pkg (10oz/300g) frozen or fresh chopped broccoli	2
3		eggs, beaten	3
1	cup	milk	250 mL
1	cup	flour	250 mL
2	Tbsp	finely chopped onion	30 mL
1	tsp	baking powder	5 mL
2	Tbsp	butter, melted	30 mL
¾	lb	cheddar cheese, grated	375 g

Preheat oven to 350°F (180°C).
Steam broccoli until partially cooked. Drain and set aside to cool.
Thoroughly mix together the next 5 ingredients. Stir in the next 2 ingredients and the broccoli. Spread evenly into a lightly oiled 9x13" (22x34cm) baking dish.
Bake for 30-35 minutes or until set.
Let stand 5 minutes. Cut into squares and serve warm.
Note: These squares freeze well and may be reheated in the microwave.
Serves a crowd.

Artichoke Squares

Follow the recipe for Broccoli Brownies, substituting for the broccoli:

3	jars (6oz/170g) artichoke hearts, drained and chopped	3

Salmon Pâté

¼	lb	smoked salmon or lox	125 g
1		pkg (8oz/250g) light cream cheese	1
2	Tbsp	chopped onion	30 mL
1	Tbsp	lemon juice	15 mL
1	Tbsp	Worcestershire sauce	15 mL

Combine all ingredients in a blender or food processor and process for a few seconds. Spoon into a pâté dish and serve with crackers. Makes 1½ cups (375mL).

Salmon Mousse

A much sought after recipe from Café Køkken in Vancouver.

1	lb	raw salmon, minced	500 g
¾	cup	sour cream	175 mL
3		eggs	3
1	Tbsp	flour	15 mL
1½	tsp	salt	7 mL
½	tsp	white pepper	2 mL
½	tsp	tarragon	2 mL
1	cup	assorted chopped herbs *eg* green onions, parsley, dill, *etc*	250 mL

Preheat oven to 350°F (180°C).
Line a 7" (17cm) long narrow bread pan with parchment paper.
Combine the first 7 ingredients and spread half in the prepared pan.
Layer with herbs. Spread with remaining salmon mixture. Place pan in a water-filled roasting pan.
Bake for 1 hour until firm.
Cool before removing from pan. Slice and serve for a buffet or place on individual lettuce-lined salad plates and serve as a starter course.
Serves 8 as an appetizer.

Seashore Tuna Dip

1		pkg (8oz/250g) cream cheese, light or regular	1
3	Tbsp	mayonnaise	45 mL
1		can (7.5oz/213g) flaked white water pack tuna fish, drained	1
½		medium onion, chopped	½
1		clove garlic, minced	1
1	Tbsp	chopped parsley	15 mL
1	tsp	Worcestershire sauce	5 mL
⅛	tsp	Tabasco sauce	.5 mL
		salt and pepper to taste	

Combine all the ingredients in a blender or food processor and blend until smooth. Serve with crackers or corn chips.
Makes approximately 2 cups (500mL).

Tangy Cottage Cheese Dip

1		bunch green onions, chopped	1
1	cup	cottage cheese	250 mL
½	cup	mayonnaise, light or regular	125 mL
2	tsp	Worcestershire sauce	10 mL
2	tsp	horseradish	10 mL
1	tsp	celery seed	5 mL
½	tsp	seasoned salt	2 mL
¼	tsp	Tabasco sauce	1 mL

Combine all ingredients in a blender or food processor and blend until smooth. Serve with fresh vegetables.
Makes approximately 2 cups (500 mL).

Coconut Shrimp

An intriguing recipe from David Dustan, Executive Chef at Lonsdale Quay Hotel in North Vancouver.

8		black tiger prawns, peeled and deveined	8
		salt and pepper to taste	
¼	cup	flour	50 mL
		beer batter	
½	cup	sweet shredded coconut	125 mL
		hot oil	
2		leaf lettuce leaves, shredded	2
½		lemon, fanned	½
⅓	cup	apricot plum sauce	75 mL

Butterfly prawns leaving tails on. Season and dredge in flour. Dip prawns into beer batter then roll into coconut as if to bread them. In a deep pan of hot oil, fry prawns until golden brown.

On two salad plates arrange lettuce on top half and pour apricot plum sauce on bottom half. Place 4 prawns on top of lettuce on each plate. Garnish with a lemon fan on the side. Bon appétit!

Serves 2.

Beer Batter

1		egg	1
¼	cup	flour	50 mL
¼	tsp	baking powder	1 mL
2	Tbsp	beer	30 mL

Beat together all the ingredients in the order given until smooth.

Apricot Plum Sauce

1		can (14oz/398mL) pitted plums	1
2	Tbsp	apricot jam	30 mL
1	Tbsp	molasses	15 mL
½	tsp	finely chopped ginger	2 mL

Process all the ingredients in a blender. Transfer to a saucepan and boil for approximately 5 minutes. Check sweetness and leave to cool.

Crêpe Appetizer

Crêpes

3		large eggs	3
¾	cup	flour	175 mL
½	tsp	salt	2 mL
1½	cups	milk	375 mL
3	Tbsp	melted butter	45 mL

Combine ingredients in a blender and process until smooth. Refrigerate for 2 hours. Heat and lightly oil a 6" (14cm) crêpe pan. When hot pour a scant ¼ cup (50mL) of batter into pan, tilting to spread batter. Cook for 1 minute, turn and cook underside until golden. Repeat with remaining batter. Crêpes may be made in advance and frozen.

Fillings

Crab

4	oz	crab	125 g
¼	cup	mayonnaise	50 mL
1	Tbsp	chopped onion	15 mL
		pepper	

Cream Cheese

4	oz	cream cheese	125 g
2	Tbsp	mayonnaise	30 mL
4		strips bacon, cooked and crumbled	4
1	Tbsp	chopped green onion	15 mL

Spread a thin layer of crab filling on a crêpe, top with a second crêpe, spread cream cheese filling over top. Repeat, layering twice more, ending with a crêpe on top. There are enough crêpes and fillings to make 2 appetizer rounds. Wrap and refrigerate for several hours. Place on a serving plate and cut each round into small wedges, securing each with a toothpick. Present garnished with parsley.
Serves 8.

Moroccan Carrot Appetizer

1	lb	carrots, peeled and cut into chunks	500 g
4	Tbsp	water	60 mL
4	Tbsp	olive oil	60 mL
2		cloves garlic, minced	2
1-2	Tbsp	vinegar	15-30 mL
¼	tsp	cayenne	1 mL
¼	tsp	cumin	1 mL
¼	tsp	paprika	1 mL
		salt and pepper	

Blanch carrots in boiling water for 1 minute. Drain. Add the next 3 ingredients and simmer until crisp tender. Drain. Add the remaining ingredients and adjust seasonings. Garnish with chopped parsley. Store in the refrigerator.
Serves 6.

California Guacamole

Spicy and awesome.

3		avocados, peeled and diced	3
3		plum tomatoes, seeded and chopped	3
3		cloves garlic, minced	3
2		scallions, minced	2
1		jalapeño pepper, cored, seeded and minced	1
3	Tbsp	lemon juice	45 mL
2	tsp	chopped cilantro	10 mL
1	tsp	Tabasco sauce	5 mL
		salt and pepper to taste	

Combine all the ingredients, serve within 2 hours with corn chips.
Makes about 2½ cups (625mL).

Chili Shrimp

Let guests do their own thing!

1	lb	prawns	500 g
½	cup	sesame seeds	125 mL

Dipping Sauce

½	cup	chili sauce	125 mL
¼	cup	hot sweet and sour sauce	50 mL
1	Tbsp	hot chili sauce (yes 1Tbsp/15mL!)	15 mL

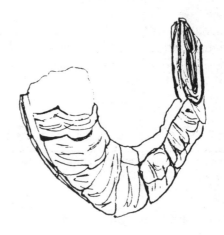

Quickly poach prawns (1-2 minutes). Cool, peel and devein. Place on a lettuce-lined plate. Combine sauce ingredients and place in a small serving bowl. Place sesame seeds in another bowl. Dip prawns in sauce and then in seeds. Enjoy!

Note: To serve as an appetizer salad, alternate 4 sauced and seeded prawns with 4 slices of avocado on lettuce-lined plates. Garnish with thin lemon slices and fresh strawberries.

Serves 6.

Soups

Wild Rice and Mushroom Soup

A great beginning for an elegant dinner.

⅓	cup	wild rice	75 mL
1		chicken bouillon cube	1
3	cups	water	750 mL
½	lb	mushrooms, sliced	250 g
1	Tbsp	oil	15 mL
1	Tbsp	flour	15 mL
3	cups	milk	750 mL

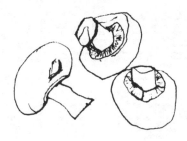

Thoroughly rinse and drain rice. Place in a small heavy saucepan, add bouillon cube and water, cover and bring to a boil. Lower heat and simmer for 45 minutes or until rice is just tender. Do not drain. Sauté mushrooms in oil over high heat until browned. Stir in flour and milk. Cook and stir until thickened. Cool slightly. Pour into a blender or a food processor and purée until smooth. Add all but ¼ cup (50mL) cooked rice to blender and continue to process until very smooth, about 5 minutes. Return to pan and heat (if soup is too thick add a little more milk). Add a small spoonful of the reserved rice to each soup bowl. Ladle hot soup over.
Serves 6.

Bouillabaisse

A favourite recipe of Ann Mortifee, entertainer.

3		leeks, chopped	3
3		cloves garlic, minced	3
2		onions, chopped	2
2		carrots, chopped	2
½	cup	olive oil	125 mL
3	cups	fish stock or water	750 mL
2	lb	assorted fish, cut in chunks	1 kg
4		tomatoes, chopped	4
1		bay leaf	1
		chopped fresh parsley, thyme, oregano, salt and pepper to taste	
2	cups	assorted shellfish *eg* shrimp, crab, lobster, *etc*	500 mL
2		tins (14oz/398mL) clams	2
½	cup	wine	125 mL
1	Tbsp	lemon juice	15 mL
1	cup	cream (optional)	250 mL

In a heavy large pot combine the first 5 ingredients and cook over medium heat until vegetables are golden. Add the next 9 ingredients, cover and simmer for 20 minutes. Add shellfish and clams and cook for 10 minutes. Stir in wine and lemon juice. Keep on low heat until serving time. Stir in cream a few minutes before serving.
Serves 8.

Cream of Avocado Soup

Light, cool and refreshing.

2		large avocados or 3 medium, peeled and quartered	2
1¾	cups	milk	425 mL
1		can (10oz/284mL) chicken broth	1
1	Tbsp	lemon juice	15 mL
½	tsp	salt	2 mL
		dash of pepper	
		dried dill for garnish	

Place the ingredients in a blender and process until smooth. Chill 5-6 hours before serving. Garnish with dill.
Serves 8.

Iced Cucumber Shrimp Soup♡

The perfect choice for a summer dinner party.

1		thin English cucumber, peeled and grated	1
2¼	cups	yogurt	550 mL
2	cups	chicken broth	500 mL
1	cup	light cream (optional)	250 mL
⅔	cup	tomato juice	150 mL
1		large clove garlic, minced	1
½	lb	cooked, shelled shrimp	250 g
⅛	tsp	Tabasco sauce	.5 mL
		fresh dill	

Thoroughly drain cucumber in a colander, about 20 minutes, and pat dry. Stir all the ingredients together, cover and chill thoroughly. Serve with a sprig of dill on top.
Serves 8-10.

Salmon Bisque

B.C. salmon stars in this recipe from Nicola Cavendish, actress.

1	lb	cooked salmon	500 g
1	cup	tomato juice	250 mL
½	cup	parsley, finely minced	125 mL
⅓	cup	chopped onion	75 mL
2	cups	water	500 mL
¼	cup	butter, melted	50 mL
¼	cup	flour	50 mL
3	cups	milk	750 mL
1½	tsp	salt	7 mL
½	tsp	paprika	2 mL

Simmer the first 5 ingredients in a saucepan for 20 minutes. Strain, reserving salmon. Blend butter and flour in a saucepan. Slowly stir in milk. Season and bring sauce to a boil. Add salmon mixture and heat through but do not boil.
Serves 6.

Chunky Pizza Soup

1	Tbsp	vegetable oil	15 mL
1		small onion, diced	1
½	cup	sliced fresh mushrooms	125 mL
¼	cup	slivered green pepper	50 mL
1		can (28oz/796mL) tomatoes, crushed	1
1	cup	beef stock	250 mL
1	cup	thinly sliced pepperoni	250 mL
½-1	tsp	dried basil	2-5 mL
1	cup	shredded mozzarella cheese	250 mL

Sauté onion, mushrooms and green pepper in oil (do not let vegetables brown). Add the next 4 ingredients and cook until heated through. Ladle into soup bowls, sprinkle with cheese and microwave on high for 2 minutes or until cheese melts.
Note: For low cholesterol diet, substitute sliced turkey weiners and low fat cheese.
Serves 4.

Mexican Carrot Soup

1		medium onion, chopped	1
2	Tbsp	butter	30 mL
3	cups	grated carrots	750 mL
4	cups	chicken stock	1 L
2	Tbsp	white rice	30 mL
1	tsp	cumin	5 mL
1	tsp	coriander	5 mL
		salt and pepper to taste	
		carrot curls and sour	
		cream for garnish	

In a large heavy saucepan, sauté onion in butter until transparent. Add the next 3 ingredients and simmer gently for 30 minutes. Allow to cool slightly and purée in blender. Reheat adding spices. Serve garnished with carrot curls and sour cream.
Serves 6.

New Orleans Sherry Bisque

1		can (10oz/284mL) green pea soup	1
1		can (10oz/284mL) mushroom soup	1
1		can (10oz/284mL) tomato soup	1
2	cups	milk	500 mL
1		can (7oz/198g) minced clams	1
¼	cup	sherry	50 mL
3	Tbsp	chopped parsley	45 mL

Mix the first 5 ingredients together and simmer for 5 minutes. Add sherry and mix well. Pour into bowls and sprinkle with parsley.
Note: Add sherry just before serving. For a different taste treat, try ½ lb (250g) shrimp or crab in place of clams.
Serves 6.

Curry Soup

This spicy soup is equally good served hot or cold and freezes well.

2		large onions, chopped	2
1	cup	chopped green pepper	250 mL
½	cup	chopped celery	125 mL
1		clove garlic, minced	1
3	Tbsp	butter	45 mL
5	cups	chicken stock	1.25 L
1	cup	chopped tart apple	250 mL
1	Tbsp	curry powder	15 mL
2	tsp	lemon juice	10 mL

Sauté the first 5 ingredients in a medium saucepan until soft, 8-10 minutes. Add stock, apple and curry powder, cover and simmer 30 minutes. Add lemon juice and cool. Pour into a blender or food processor and purée until smooth. Serve hot or cold garnished with watercress or parsley.
Serves 6.

Tomato and Red Pepper Soup

The flavour of summer enhanced with balsamic vinegar.

2		large sweet red peppers	2
2		large tomatoes	2
2	cups	chopped red onion	500 mL
2		cloves garlic, minced	2
2	Tbsp	olive oil	30 mL
2	cups	chicken stock	500 mL
¼	tsp	thyme	1 mL
1		bay leaf	1
⅛	tsp	cayenne pepper	.5 mL
1½	Tbsp	balsamic vinegar	22 mL
		salt and pepper to taste	

Preheat oven to 375°F (190°C).
Roast tomatoes and peppers for 45 minutes. Remove from oven and press through a food mill or sieve. In a large saucepan cook onion and garlic in oil until translucent, but not brown. Add the next 4 ingredients and the tomato and pepper liquid. Simmer covered for 20 minutes. Remove bay leaf and purée in blender or food processor. Add vinegar, salt and pepper.
Serves 4-6.

Beef Vegetable Soup

This winter favourite is from Barbara McQuade, food editor at the Vancouver Sun.

1	cup	dried small white beans	250 mL
1	Tbsp	vegetable oil	15 mL
1	lb	ground beef	500 g
1	cup	coarse-chopped onion	250 mL
1		large clove garlic, minced	1
10	cups	beef broth	2½ L
2	Tbsp	tomato paste	30 mL
1½	cups	coarsely-shredded cabbage	375 mL
4		medium tomatoes, peeled, seeded and chopped	4
2		carrots, sliced thinly	2
1	cup	macaroni	250 mL
½	tsp	dried oregano	2 mL
½	tsp	dried basil	2 mL
2		small zucchini, sliced thinly	2
		salt & fresh ground pepper	
⅓	cup	grated parmesan cheese	75 mL

Place beans in a bowl; cover with boiling water and let stand for 1 hour. Drain beans. Heat oil in a heavy 5 quart (5L) saucepan and add beef, onion and garlic; cook until meat is no longer pink. Drain off fat. Add beans and beef broth; cover and simmer about 1 hour or until beans are tender. Stir a few tablespoons of hot broth into tomato paste, then stir into soup. Add the next 6 ingredients and simmer 15 minutes. Add zucchini and simmer 5 minutes. Season to taste and serve soup sprinkled with parmesan cheese.
Serves 8-10.

Cheese Vegetable Soup

2½	cups	water	625 mL
1		bouillon cube	1
1	cup	cubed potato	250 mL
½	cup	sliced carrots	125 mL
½	cup	chopped celery	125 mL
2½	cups	milk	625 mL
½	cup	minced onion	125 mL
¼	cup	flour	50 mL
¼	cup	butter	50 mL
¼	tsp	baking powder	1 mL
¼	tsp	paprika	1 mL
		salt and pepper to taste	
4	oz	sharp cheddar cheese, cubed	125 g
1	Tbsp	chopped parsley	15 mL

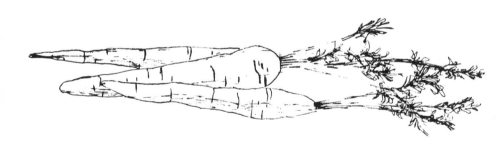

Place the first 5 ingredients in a saucepan and cook until vegetables are tender. Set aside. Combine the next 8 ingredients in a blender and process until smooth. Pour into a large heavy saucepan and cook over medium heat until thickened. Add cooked vegetables (including water) and cheese and heat through. Serve garnished with parsley. Note: For a smooth cream soup, process once more in the blender. Serves 6.

Zucchini, Leek, Tomato Soup

2	tsp	vegetable oil	10 mL
4		leeks, cleaned and chopped (white and light green parts only)	4
1		small onion, chopped	1
2		medium zucchini, chopped	2
4	cups	beef or chicken broth	1 L
1		can (28oz/796mL) stewed tomatoes	1
4	tsp	dry sherry	20 mL
½	tsp	dried dill	2 mL
½	tsp	dried oregano	2 mL
½	tsp	pepper	2 mL
		salt to taste	

Garnish

croutons (optional)
sour cream (optional)

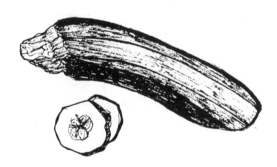

In a large saucepan gently cook leeks and onion in oil for 5 minutes, stirring frequently. Add zucchini and continue cooking for 10 minutes. Stir in the remaining ingredients and simmer for 45 minutes. Serve sprinkled with a few croutons and a little sour cream if desired.
Serves 8.

Gazpacho

A classic summer soup.

1	cup	finely chopped blanched tomatoes	250 mL
½	cup	diced green pepper	125 mL
½	cup	diced celery	125 mL
½	cup	diced green onion	125 mL
½	cup	diced cucumber	125 mL
3	Tbsp	chopped parsley	45 mL
2		cloves garlic, minced	2
4	cups	V-8 juice	1 L
3	Tbsp	tarragon vinegar	45 mL
2	Tbsp	red wine vinegar	30 mL
2	Tbsp	olive oil	30 mL
1	tsp	dried basil	5 mL
1	tsp	salt	5 mL
½	tsp	Worcestershire sauce	2 mL
¼	tsp	black pepper	1 mL
¼	tsp	Tabasco sauce	1 mL

Combine all the ingredients in a large glass bowl. Cover and refrigerate overnight. Sprinkle with chopped cucumber, onion, green pepper and croutons before serving.

Note: ½ lb (250g) shrimp may be added for variety.

Serves 6.

Borscht

2	cups	water	500 mL
2	cups	chopped, peeled beets	500 mL
1	cup	chopped onion	250 mL
½	cup	chopped carrot	125 mL
½	cup	chopped celery	125 mL
2	cups	soup stock (beef, chicken or vegetable)	500 mL
1	cup	tomato juice	250 mL
½	cup	chopped cabbage	125 mL
½	cup	shredded beet tops	125 mL
		salt, pepper and dill to taste	
2		new potatoes, cut in chunks	2
1	cup	sour cream	250 mL

In a large pot combine the first 5 ingredients and cook until tender. Add the next 4 ingredients and simmer for 15 minutes. Season. Boil potatoes until tender, in a separate pot to avoid discolouring. Drain and add to beet mixture along with sour cream. Stir to blend but do not boil. Garnish with a dollop of sour cream and sprinkle with dill. Serves 6.

Minestrone Soup

Hearty and delicious.

1	cup	cubed zucchini	250 mL
½	cup	chopped onion	125 mL
½	cup	sliced celery	125 mL
1		clove garlic, crushed	1
3	Tbsp	oil	45 mL
8	cups	chicken stock	2 L
1		can (5½oz/156mL) tomato paste	1
1	cup	coarsely chopped cabbage	250 mL
¾	cup	sliced green beans	175 mL
¾	cup	diced carrots	175 mL
1		medium potato, diced	1
1	Tbsp	chopped fresh parsley	15 mL
¼	tsp	basil	1 mL
¼	tsp	celery seed	1 mL
		salt and pepper to taste	
4	oz	uncooked spaghetti, broken in quarters	125 g

Sauté the first 4 ingredients in oil until onion is transparent. Add chicken stock, tomato paste, vegetables and seasonings. Bring to a boil. Reduce heat and simmer until vegetables are almost tender, about 20 minutes. Add spaghetti and simmer until tender, about 10 minutes.

Note: For variety, 1 cup cooked navy beans may be added at the same time as spaghetti.

Serves 6-8.

Tomato and Basil Soup

1		large onion, coarsely chopped	1
1		carrot, grated	1
2	Tbsp	butter	30 mL
5		medium, ripe tomatoes, peeled and quartered	5
¼	cup	finely chopped fresh basil	50 mL
¾	tsp	sugar	3 mL
½	tsp	ground pepper	2 mL
¼	tsp	salt	1 mL
2	cups	chicken stock	500 mL

In a large saucepan sauté onion and carrot in butter until onion is soft. Stir in the next 5 ingredients, cover and simmer for 15 minutes. Purée in a blender until smooth. Return purée to saucepan, add stock and reheat.
Serves 4-6.

Tipsy Soup

2		cans (10oz/284mL) bisque of tomato soup	2
1		can (10oz/284mL) consommé	1
1		can (14oz/398mL) Italian plum tomatoes, broken up	1
1	tsp	Worcestershire sauce garlic powder to taste	5 mL
2½	oz	Vodka	75 mL

Combine the first 5 ingredients together and heat through. Add Vodka just before serving.
Soup may be garnished with a dob of sour cream, fresh basil or parsley and/or croutons.
Serves 6-8.

Apple Celery Soup

A treat for celery fans.

1½	lb	apples, peeled, cored and chopped	750 g
1	lb	celery, chopped	500 g
2	Tbsp	butter	30 mL
4	cups	chicken broth	1 L
1		can (14oz/398mL) tomatoes	1
½	tsp	ground pepper	2 mL
¼	cup	yogurt	50 mL
2	Tbsp	chopped parsley	30 mL

Cook apples and celery in butter over low heat until limp. Add the next 3 ingredients, cover and simmer for 25 minutes. Purée in a blender or a food processor. Strain. Serve with a dollop of yogurt and a sprinkling of parsley.
Serves 6.

Scots' Broth

10	cups	water	2.5 L
2	lb	lamb shanks	1 kg
1	cup	dried split peas	250 mL
½	cup	pot barley	125 mL
1		large onion, sliced	1
1		large leek, white part only, sliced	1
2		medium turnips, peeled and diced	2
3		carrots, diced	3
1		small cabbage, shredded	1
2	Tbsp	chopped parsley	30 mL
		salt and pepper to taste	

Bring the water, meat and dried peas to a boil. Skim the top, cover and simmer gently for 1 hour. Remove shanks and dice meat. Return meat to pan, discarding bones. Add the next 5 ingredients and simmer an additional 20 minutes. Add cabbage, parsley and seasonings. Simmer for 15 minutes.
Serves 8.

Salads

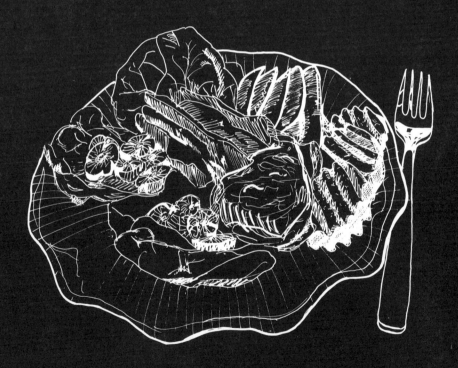

Yaki Soba Turkey Salad

Hot turkey over cold crisp greens - delightful!

1		head romaine lettuce, torn in pieces	1
4		medium sized tomatoes, cut in bite size pieces	4
1		red pepper, sliced (or a combination of peppers)	1
1		can (14oz/398mL) unsweetened pineapple chunks, drained	1
2		large turkey cutlets	2
1	Tbsp	vegetable oil	15 mL
1	cup	pea pods (optional)	250 mL

Arrange lettuce on 4 plates. Top with tomatoes, pineapple chunks and pepper strips. Set aside. Slice turkey into thin strips and marinate in a little dressing, using just enough to coat meat. Heat oil in a wok or heavy pan and sauté turkey until just cooked. Add pea pods and sauté 1 minute. Add remaining dressing and heat. Spoon over lettuce and sprinkle with almonds and sesame seeds. Serves 4.

Dressing

1		clove garlic, minced	1
½"		slice fresh ginger, minced	1 cm
¼	cup	vegetable oil	50 mL
3	Tbsp	soy sauce	45 mL
3	Tbsp	saki or dry sherry	45 mL
3	Tbsp	rice wine vinegar	45 mL
½-1	tsp	sambal oelek	2-5 mL
½	tsp	sesame oil	2 mL

Combine dressing ingredients and shake well.

Crab and Grapefruit Salad

A spectacular first course or luncheon salad.

12	oz	crabmeat	375 g
2		grapefruit, peeled and cut in sections	2
4		romaine lettuce leaves	4
½	cup	honey lemon dressing	125 mL
4		tomato wedges	4
4		lemon wedges	4
12		black olives	12
1	tsp	chopped fresh parsley	5 mL

Place one lettuce leaf on each serving plate. Toss crabmeat, ½ of the grapefruit sections and ½ cup (125mL) dressing. Arrange this mixture on the lettuce. Sprinkle parsley and remaining grapefruit on top. Garnish each salad with a tomato and lemon wedge, three black olives and a parsley sprig.

Honey Lemon Dressing

¼	cup	lemon juice	50 mL
1	Tbsp	honey	15 mL
¼	tsp	ground celery seed	1 mL
¼	tsp	seasoned salt	1 mL
¼	tsp	ground white pepper	1 mL
⅛	tsp	mustard	.5 mL
⅛	tsp	dried dill	.5 mL
½	cup	sunflower seed oil	125 mL

In a blender or food processor combine the first 7 ingredients. Blend for 30 seconds. With the motor running add oil very slowly in a thin steady stream until thick and creamy. Refrigerate until ready to use. Serves 4.

Shrimp Boats

A light and luscious summertime salad suitable for lunch or dinner.

½	cup	light mayonnaise	125 mL
½	cup	plain light yogurt	125 mL
2	tsp	lemon juice	10 mL
1	tsp	curry powder	5 mL
½	tsp	lemon pepper	2 mL
½	lb	fresh shrimp	250 g
2	cups	green grapes, halved	500 mL
2		cantaloupes, halved and seeded	2
		mint sprigs or lemon twists for garnish	
		lettuce leaves	

Mix together the first 5 ingredients. Stir in the shrimp and grapes. Spoon mixture into cantaloupe halves. Garnish with a sprig of fresh mint or lemon twists and serve on a bed of lettuce.
Serves 4.

Shrimp and Asparagus Salad

1½	lb	asparagus	750 g
1	lb	shrimp	500 g
⅓	cup	sliced green onions	75 mL
2	Tbsp	chopped parsley	30 mL
1		medium lemon, very thinly sliced	1
3		medium tomatoes, peeled and chopped	3
2		heads butter lettuce	2

Dressing

¼	cup	vegetable oil	50 mL
3	Tbsp	dry white wine	45 mL
2	Tbsp	lemon juice	30 mL
1	Tbsp	sugar	15 mL
1	Tbsp	fresh chopped basil	15 mL
1	tsp	salt	5 mL
¼	tsp	pepper	1 mL
¼	tsp	Tabasco sauce	1 mL

Blanch asparagus in boiling water for 1 minute. Plunge into ice water. Drain and cut into ½" (1.3cm) diagonal pieces. Toss with the next 4 ingredients. Combine dressing ingredients, pour over first mixture, cover and chill for 3-4 hours. Add tomatoes and toss. Drain and serve on a bed of butter lettuce leaves.

Note: Green beans may be substituted when asparagus is not available.

Serves 6.

Papaya and Crab Salad

A delicious luncheon entrée.

1	cup	snow peas	250 mL
1		papaya, peeled and cubed	1
½	lb	crabmeat	250 g
1		kiwi fruit, peeled	1
2	Tbsp	light mayonnaise	30 mL
½	tsp	brandy (optional)	2 mL
		lettuce leaves	
		cherry tomatoes	
		lemon wedges	

Blanch snow peas in boiling water for 30 seconds. Drain and chill. Toss papaya with crabmeat and place on a bed of lettuce. Garnish with snow peas, cherry tomatoes and a lemon wedge. Combine kiwi fruit, mayonnaise and brandy in a blender and process until smooth. Drizzle over salads.
Serves 4 as a salad, 2 as an entrée.

Wild Rice and Prawn Salad

A delicious and different first course or entrée.

4	cups	chicken stock	1 L
½	cup	wild rice, rinsed	125 mL
1	lb	prawns, cooked	500 g
¼	lb	small mushrooms, sliced	125 g
4		shallots, chopped	4
1		red pepper, sliced	1
2		large spinach leaves, shredded	2
		dressing	
		butter lettuce leaves	

Bring stock to a boil in a pan, add rice and simmer uncovered for 40 minutes or until tender. Drain. Shell and devein prawns and mix into rice along with mushrooms, shallots, red pepper and spinach. Add dressing and toss to coat. Refrigerate for 2 hours before serving. Serve on lettuce-lined plates.
Serves 6-8 as an appetizer.

Dressing

⅓	cup	olive oil	75 mL
2	Tbsp	lemon juice	30 mL
2	tsp	Dijon mustard	10 mL
¼	tsp	pepper	1 mL
¼	tsp	ground celery seed	1 mL

Combine the dressing ingredients in a jar. Cover and shake well to blend.

Bell Pepper Slaw

A refreshing new twist for an old standby.

1		each sweet red, yellow, orange and green bell pepper	1
2	cups	shredded cabbage	500 mL
½	cup	vinegar	125 mL
½	cup	oil	125 mL
1	Tbsp	sugar	15 mL
1	Tbsp	Dijon mustard	15 mL
½	tsp	salt	2 mL
¼	tsp	pepper	1 mL
¼	tsp	celery seed	1 mL

Quarter and seed peppers and cut into very thin strips, combine with cabbage. Thoroughly blend together the remaining ingredients. Pour over cabbage and pepper mixture. Cover tightly and refrigerate at least 1 hour.
Serves 6.

Zucchini Apple Slaw

Quick and delicious.

½	cup	light mayonnaise	125 mL
3	Tbsp	cider vinegar	45 mL
2	tsp	sugar	10 mL
1	tsp	caraway or sesame seeds	5 mL
4	cups	coarsely shredded zucchini	1 L
¼	cup	thinly sliced green onion	50 mL
2		green or red tart apples, cored and diced	2

Combine the first 4 ingredients to make dressing and set aside. Toss together the next 3 ingredients. Pour the dressing over and toss thoroughly. Garnish plates with three or four thin slices of zucchini.
Serves 6.

Ruby Salad

A wonderful make ahead salad.

1		large red cabbage, grated or shredded	1	
1		large Spanish onion, chopped	1	
3-4		carrots, grated	3-4	
½	cup	white sugar	125	mL
1	cup	white wine vinegar	250	mL
⅔	cup	vegetable oil	150	mL
1	Tbsp	salt	15	mL
1	tsp	dry mustard	5	mL
1	tsp	celery seed	5	mL

Combine the vegetables in a large bowl. Sprinkle the sugar over. Heat the remaining ingredients and stir to blend. Pour over vegetables, mixing thoroughly. Cover and refrigerate several hours before serving. This will keep in the refrigerator for 6 weeks. Serves 12.

Red and Green Cashew Salad

A delightful summer salad that's also perfect for Christmas.

1	lb	broccoli florets	500	g
½	lb	cherry tomatoes, halved	250	g
4		green onions, chopped	4	
1	cup	roasted cashews	250	mL
		ranch style dressing (page 54)		

Cut broccoli in bite-size pieces, add tomatoes, onions and cashews. Toss with dressing. If made ahead add cashews just before serving. Serves 8.

Strawberry Nut Spinach Salad

Popeye never knew spinach like this!

1	lb	fresh spinach, stemmed, washed, dried and torn in pieces	500 g
2	cups	sliced fresh strawberries	500 mL
1		small red onion, thinly sliced (optional)	1
½	cup	slivered almonds, toasted	125 mL

Toss the spinach and strawberries in a large bowl. Chill if made ahead. Pour the dressing over just before serving and toss well to coat. Sprinkle the almonds over and gently toss.

Dressing

½	cup	oil	125 mL
¼	cup	vinegar	50 mL
¼	cup	sugar	50 mL
2	Tbsp	toasted sesame seeds	30 mL
2	Tbsp	finely chopped onion	30 mL
1	Tbsp	poppy seeds	15 mL
¼	tsp	paprika	1 mL

Combine the dressing ingredients and refrigerate to chill.
Serves 6-8.

Endive and Snow Pea Salad

3	Tbsp	red wine vinegar	45 mL
2	Tbsp	Dijon mustard	30 mL
1	Tbsp	olive oil	15 mL
¼	tsp	salt	1 mL
⅛	tsp	freshly ground pepper	.5 mL
½	cup	olive oil	125 mL
3	Tbsp	chopped green onion	45 mL
¾	lb	snow peas, ends trimmed and strings removed	375 g
4		heads Belgian endive	4
1	cup	bean sprouts (optional)	250 mL
2	Tbsp	sesame seeds, toasted	30 mL

In a blender combine the first 5 ingredients. Very slowly add the oil until mixture is the consistency of mayonnaise. Stir in onion. Cover and let stand at room temperature up to 8 hours. Blanch peas in a pot of boiling water for 1 minute. Drain and plunge into ice water to cool. Drain and dry. Place in a salad bowl. Cut endives in half lengthwise, then sliver halves lengthwise. Add to peas with remaining ingredients. Pour dressing over and toss to coat. Sprinkle with sesame seeds.
Serves 8.

Polynesian Salad

1	cup	rice	250 mL
6	oz	shrimp	170 g
3		celery stalks, sliced	3
4		green onions, chopped	4
1¼	cups	frozen peas	300 mL
2	cups	chow mein noodles	500 mL
½		green pepper, slivered (optional)	½

Dressing

½	cup	olive or vegetable oil	125 mL
¼	cup	soy sauce	50 mL
3	Tbsp	vinegar	45 mL
2	tsp	curry powder	10 mL
1	tsp	sugar	5 mL
1	tsp	celery seed	5 mL
½	tsp	ginger	2 mL

Cook rice. Cool. Add shrimp, celery and onions. Mixture may be refrigerated at this point. Add peas ½ hour before serving. Combine dressing ingredients and pour over salad just before serving. Add noodles and toss.
Serves 6.

Three Layer Jelly Salad

Perfect for that special occasion.

First Layer

1		pkg (3oz/85g) lime gelatin	1
1	cup	boiling water	250 mL
1		can (14oz/398mL) crushed pineapple and juice	1

Second Layer

1		pkg (3oz/85g) lemon gelatin	1
¾	cup	boiling water	175 mL
1	cup	cottage cheese	250 mL
1		pkg (4oz/125g) cream cheese	1
1	cup	whipping cream, whipped	250 mL

Third Layer

1		pkg (3oz/85g) raspberry gelatin	1
1½	cups	boiling water	375 mL

First Layer
Dissolve gelatin in boiling water. Add pineapple and let set in a 9x13" (22x34cm) glass dish.

Second Layer
Dissolve gelatin in boiling water and let partially set. Beat gelatin. Beat cheeses together, then fold in whipped cream and gelatin. Spread on first layer. Let set.

Third Layer
Dissolve gelatin in boiling water. Let cool. Pour over second layer. Let set.
To serve, cut into small squares.
Serves 24-28.

Marinated Bean Salad

Great for cottages or boating.

1		can (19oz/540mL) red kidney beans	1
1		can (19oz/540mL) white kidney beans	1
1		can (19oz/540mL) broad or lima beans	1
1		can (19oz/540mL) garbanzo beans or chick peas	1
1		large onion, chopped	1
1		green pepper, chopped	1
⅔	cup	olive oil	150 mL
⅔	cup	red wine vinegar	150 mL
2	Tbsp	sugar	30 mL
		salt and pepper to taste	

Drain all the beans and combine the first 6 ingredients in a large bowl. Mix together the remaining ingredients to make dressing. Pour over bean mixture and combine. Cover and refrigerate several hours. Will keep several days refrigerated.
Serves 10-12.

Peanut Potato Salad

2	lb	red new potatoes, cooked drained and cubed	1 kg
½	cup	chopped green pepper	125 mL
½	cup	chopped celery	125 mL
¾	cup	thinly sliced green onion	175 mL
¼	cup	chopped parsley	50 mL
¼	cup	diced cucumber or zucchini	50 mL
¾	cup	Spanish peanuts, divided	175 mL
½	cup	mayonnaise	125 mL
2	Tbsp	cider vinegar	30 mL
1	Tbsp	chunk style peanut butter	15 mL
1	tsp	Dijon mustard	5 mL
½	tsp	curry powder (optional)	2 mL
¼	tsp	ground pepper several drops of Tabasco sauce	1 mL

Combine the first 6 ingredients and ½ cup (125mL) peanuts. In a small bowl stir together the next 7 ingredients. Pour over potato mixture and mix well. Cover and chill several hours or overnight. Stir well before serving and garnish with remaining nuts.
Serves 6-8.

Warm Goat Cheese Salad

A very popular recipe from Michel Jacob, chef owner of Le Crocodile restaurant in Vancouver.

1		hard, log shaped goat cheese	1
		at least 6" (15cm) long	
		water	
½	cup	breadcrumbs	125 mL
2	Tbsp	butter	30 mL
1	Tbsp	Dijon mustard	15 mL
¾	cup	vegetable oil	175 mL
¼	cup	white wine vinegar	50 mL
1	tsp	lemon juice	5 mL
		salt and pepper to taste	
1		large head of curly endive	1

Slice the goat cheese into 6 (1"/2.5cm) thick slices. Wet each side of the slices with a little water and press into the breadcrumbs. Melt the butter in a frying pan and fry the cheese slices for 2 minutes on each side or until breadcrumbs turn a light golden colour. Set aside keeping the slices warm. Place the mustard in a medium sized bowl. Whisking continuously, add the oil, vinegar, lemon juice, salt and pepper. Toss the endive leaves in the vinaigrette and place on six individual salad plates. Top each with a warm slice of goat cheese. Serves 6.

Tabouli

An authentic Lebanese parsley salad.

2		large tomatoes, finely chopped	2
½	cup	bulgar wheat, washed and drained	125 mL
6		large bunches parsley	6
1		bunch mint	1
6-8		green onions, finely chopped	6-8
⅓	cup	olive oil	75 mL
		juice of 2 lemons	
		salt and pepper to taste	

In a bowl place tomatoes on top of wheat and let stand for 20 minutes to soften wheat. Remove stems from parsley and mint and chop leaves in a food processor, being careful not to pulverize. Combine all ingredients, mixing thoroughly. Serve in a salad bowl or on individual salad plates garnished with endive.
Serves 6-8.

Vietnamese Salad Rolls

Now you can prepare your own at home!

16-20		rounds of rice paper	16-20
¼	lb	rice vermicelli, cut in half	125 g
1	Tbsp	vinegar	15 mL
½	cup	chopped green onion	125 mL
½	cup	grated carrot	125 mL
¼	cup	finely chopped celery	50 mL
½	lb	shrimp, crab or chopped cooked chicken	250 g
½	cup	toasted peanuts	125 mL

Cook the vermicelli in a large pot of boiling water for 4-5 minutes or until tender. Drain and rinse well. Fill a large bowl with hot water and add vinegar. Place one sheet of rice paper in hot water until slightly soft. Carefully remove from water and place on a clean flat surface. Place a small portion of noodles in centre of paper and add a small portion of each of the remaining ingredients. Fold in the sides of the rice paper, then roll up from open end. Place seam side down on a plate. Repeat with remaining paper and fillings. Serve with peanut sauce.
Makes 16-20 rolls.

Peanut Sauce

½	cup	peanut butter	125 mL
1		small red chili, seeded and chopped	1
5	Tbsp	soy sauce	75 mL
5	Tbsp	coconut milk or water for thinning	75 mL

Place peanut butter, chili and soy sauce in a blender and process until smooth. Add liquid slowly to give the desired consistency.

Cherry Tomatoes with Basil

¼	cup	olive oil	50 mL
¼	cup	French walnut oil	50 mL
2	Tbsp	white wine vinegar	30 mL
1	tsp	Dijon mustard	5 mL
		salt to taste	
		freshly ground black pepper	
⅔	cup	fresh chopped & bruised basil	150 mL
5	cups	cherry tomatoes	1.25 L
		(1½lb/750g)	

Mix together the first 6 ingredients. Add basil. Add tomatoes and toss in the mixture from time to time for about one hour before serving.
Do not chill or the flavour will be spoiled.
Note: This dressing is excellent poured over thickly sliced tomatoes.
Serves 6.

Oriental Sesame Dressing

½	cup	rice wine vinegar	125 mL
3	Tbsp	vegetable oil	45 mL
2	Tbsp	soy sauce	30 mL
2	Tbsp	sugar	30 mL
2	Tbsp	sesame seeds, toasted	30 mL
1	Tbsp	minced fresh ginger	15 mL

Combine all the ingredients in a jar. Cover and shake well to blend.
Makes ¾ cup (175mL) dressing.

Sour Sweet Lime Coulis

A refreshing dressing for shrimp.

⅓	cup	fresh lime juice	75 mL
1-2	Tbsp	orange marmalade	15-30 mL
1	tsp	grated lime rind	5 mL
½	tsp	salt	2 mL
⅓	cup	olive oil	75 mL

Combine the first 4 ingredients in a blender. Process, adding oil in a thin stream. Drizzle over shrimp in a cocktail or use as a coulis under prawns.
Makes approximately ⅔ cup (150mL).

Ranch Style Dressing

1	cup	buttermilk	250 mL
⅓	cup	mayonnaise	75 mL
2	Tbsp	chopped parsley	30 mL
2		cloves garlic, minced	2
2	tsp	chopped fresh dill	10 mL
½	tsp	sugar	2 mL
¼	tsp	dry mustard	1 mL
¼	tsp	ground celery seed	1 mL
¼	tsp	fresh ground pepper	1 mL
		several drops Tabasco sauce	

Combine all ingredients and mix thoroughly. Cover and refrigerate. Will keep for 2 weeks.
Makes 1½ cups (375mL).

Florentine Snapper Rolls

Flounder, bass or sole fillets may be substituted in this delicious entrée.

4		(5oz/140g) snapper fillets	4
2	tsp	lemon juice	10 mL
		salt and pepper	
1		pkg (10oz/300g) spinach, cooked and squeezed dry	1
½	cup	sour cream	125 mL
2	Tbsp	minced onion	30 mL
2	Tbsp	minced parsley	30 mL
½	tsp	garlic powder	2 mL
⅛	tsp	pepper	.5 mL
1	Tbsp	butter, melted	15 mL
2	tsp	breadcrumbs	10 mL

Preheat oven to 375° (190°C).

Sprinkle fillets with lemon juice, salt and pepper. In a bowl mix together the next 6 ingredients. Place this filling on the lower third of each fillet and roll up. Place fillets in a greased 9" (23cm) casserole dish, drizzle with butter and sprinkle with crumbs.

Bake for 20 minutes or until fish is no longer translucent at the thickest part.

Serves 4.

Halibut and Pepper Julienne ♡

A colourful potpourri of peppers crowns fresh halibut.

4-6		halibut steaks or fillets, poached or steamed	4-6
1		red pepper, cut in thin strips	1
1		green pepper, cut in thin strips	1
½		yellow pepper, cut in thin strips	½
1		onion, sliced	1
2		stalks celery, thinly sliced	2
2	Tbsp	butter	30 mL
1		tomato, coarsely chopped	1
1	tsp	chopped parsley	5 mL
		dash of paprika, curry, cayenne, salt and pepper	
⅔	cup	white wine	150 mL

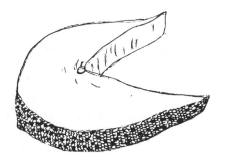

In a skillet over medium heat toss peppers, onion and celery in butter. Add remaining ingredients, except halibut, and simmer a few minutes until crisp tender. Spoon vegetables and pan juices over halibut and serve.
Serves 4-6.

Baked Salmon Fillet

3	lb	salmon fillet	1.5 kg
		salt and pepper to taste	
2	Tbsp	lemon juice	30 mL
		fresh or dried dill to taste	
½		onion, sliced very thinly	½
⅓	cup	light mayonnaise or yogurt	75 mL
		paprika	

Preheat oven to 425°F (220°C).
Place salmon in a baking dish. Cover with remaining ingredients in the order given.
Bake for 20 minutes.
Serves 6.

Broiled Fish Fillets

½	cup	parmesan cheese	125 mL
¼	cup	plain yogurt	50 mL
¼	cup	mayonnaise, light or regular	50 mL
¼	cup	melted butter	50 mL
4		green onions, chopped	4
2	Tbsp	lemon juice	30 mL
		dash of Tabasco sauce	
2	lb	fish fillets	1 kg

Preheat broiler.
Thoroughly blend the first 7 ingredients. Set aside. Dry fish with paper towels. Place in a lightly oiled baking dish and broil 4" from heat for a few minutes. Remove dish from oven and pour yogurt mixture over fish. Return to broiler and broil until golden.
Serves 6.

Shrimp Sauced Sole Rolls

Prepare this dish early in the day and slip it in the oven just before serving.

8		sole strips	8
½	lb	shrimp	250 g
1	Tbsp	butter	15 mL
1	Tbsp	flour	15 mL
1	cup	milk	250 mL
¼	tsp	salt	1 mL
¼	tsp	ground white pepper	1 mL
¾	cup	grated cheddar cheese	175 mL
½		lemon, thinly sliced	½

Preheat oven to 325°F (160°C).
Split each sole strip down the centre lengthwise. Roll up each strip and secure with a toothpick. Place rolls on a piece of heavy duty foil. Bring foil edges together and seal by folding over several times. Double fold ends of packet together. Drop into a pot of boiling water. Reduce heat and simmer 10 minutes. Carefully remove sole and place in a shallow baking dish. Slip out toothpicks. Make sauce by melting butter in a heavy saucepan. Stir in flour and cook a few seconds. Slowly stir in milk. Cook over low heat until thickened. Stir in seasonings and shrimp. Pour over sole. Sprinkle with cheese and garnish with lemon.
Bake for 15 minutes or until bubbly.
Serves 4-6 depending on size of sole pieces.

Wild Rice Seafood Casserole

¾	cup	white rice	175 mL
¾	cup	wild rice	175 mL
½	lb	shrimp	250 g
½	lb	crab	250 g
1	cup	chopped onion	250 mL
1	cup	chopped celery	250 mL
½	cup	chopped mushrooms	125 mL
¼	cup	chopped green pepper	50 mL
2	Tbsp	butter	30 mL
1		can (10oz/284mL) mushroom soup	1
⅓	cup	slivered almonds	75 mL

Preheat oven to 350°F (180°C).
Cook each rice according to package directions. Sauté onion, celery, mushrooms and green pepper in butter for 3 minutes. Combine with seafood, cooked rice and soup and place in a greased 3 qt (3L) casserole.
Bake covered for 45 minutes. The last 10 minutes, uncover and sprinkle with almonds.
Serves 6.

Shrimp in Tomato Sauce

A dieter's delight.

2		onions, sliced	2
2	Tbsp	butter	30 mL
½	cup	instant non-fat dry milk	125 mL
2	Tbsp	flour	30 mL
1		can (19oz/540mL) tomatoes	1
		salt and pepper to taste	
		curry powder (optional)	
1	lb	shrimp, fresh or frozen	500 g

In a medium saucepan sauté onions in butter. Thoroughly combine the next 6 ingredients and add to onions. Cook and stir until mixture thickens. Add shrimp and heat through. Serve with rice or pasta.
Note: This dish can be prepared with any lean fish.
Serves 4.

Pecan Chicken

Truly fast and fantastic.

4		whole chicken breasts	4
		halved, skinned and deboned	
3½	oz	ground pecans	100 g
1	cup	Dijon mustard	250 mL
¼	cup	vegetable oil	50 mL

Preheat oven to 350°F (180°C).
Whip vegetable oil with mustard. Dip each piece of chicken in mustard mixture and roll in ground pecans. Arrange in a lightly oiled baking dish.
Bake for 1 hour.
Serves 6.

Chicken Dijon

2		whole chicken breasts, boned, skinned and cubed	2
½	cup	minced green onions	125 mL
6		mushrooms, sliced	6
3	Tbsp	light margarine, divided	45 mL
⅓	cup	white wine	75 mL
2	tsp	Dijon mustard	10 mL
½	tsp	salt	2 mL
¼	tsp	garlic powder	1 mL
¼	tsp	allspice	1 mL

Sauté onions and mushrooms in half the margarine. Remove and set aside. Add remaining margarine and chicken cubes and cook until chicken turns white and is cooked through. Combine remaining ingredients, and add to pan along with onions and mushrooms. Heat through and serve.
Serves 4.

Chicken Parmesan

3		chicken breasts, skinned, boned and halved	3
1	cup	fresh breadcrumbs	250 mL
½	cup	grated parmesan cheese	125 mL
1	Tbsp	chopped parsley	15 mL
3		strips bacon, cooked and crumbled	3
6	Tbsp	butter	90 mL
2		cloves garlic, minced	2
1	tsp	Worcestershire sauce	5 mL
½	tsp	dry mustard	2 mL

Preheat oven to 325°F (160°C).
Combine the breadcrumbs, cheese, parsley and bacon and set aside.
Heat the last 4 ingredients in a saucepan, stirring until butter melts.
Dip chicken in butter mixture and place in a shallow pan. Divide the crumb mixture and place on top of each chicken piece.
Bake uncovered for 20-25 minutes. Serve with Basil Sauce.
Serves 6.

Basil Sauce

1	cup	fresh basil leaves, finely chopped	250 mL
⅓	cup	oil	75 mL
⅓	cup	cream	75 mL
¼	cup	white vinegar	50 mL
1		clove garlic, crushed	1
1		egg yolk	1
		salt and pepper to taste	

Combine the first 5 ingredients in a saucepan. Stir until heated through. Add egg yolk, stirring until sauce thickens. Do not boil. Season with salt and pepper.
Note: Try this sauce with grilled lamb chops - a pleasant change from mint sauce.

Sweet and Sour Chicken

2	lb	chicken breast, cubed	1 kg
2	Tbsp	oil	30 mL
1		medium onion, coarsely chopped	1
1		green pepper, coarsely chopped	1
3		stalks celery, sliced diagonally	3
1		can (14oz/398mL) pineapple tidbits, drained	1
½	cup	whole roasted almonds	125 mL

Sauce

¼	cup	sugar	50 mL
¼	cup	red wine vinegar	50 mL
¼	cup	chicken broth	50 mL
4	tsp	cornstarch	20 mL
1	Tbsp	soy sauce	15 mL
2	tsp	ketchup	10 mL
½	tsp	ground ginger	2 mL
¼	tsp	coriander	1 mL
¼	tsp	Tabasco sauce	1 mL
		salt to taste	

In a skillet or wok, stir fry the chicken in oil until no longer pink. Remove and add the vegetables, cooking until crisp tender. Add the pineapple and chicken. Combine all the sauce ingredients and add to the wok, cooking until thickened. Add the almonds and toss to warm. Serve immediately.
Serves 4-6.

Oat and Sesame Chicken

Moist chicken under a crispy coating.

1	cup	uncooked oat bran	250 mL
¼	cup	sesame seeds	50 mL
2	tsp	paprika	10 mL
½	tsp	salt	2 mL
¼	tsp	pepper	1 mL
2		large egg whites	2
¼	cup	buttermilk	50 mL
6		chicken breast halves, skinned and boned	6
4	Tbsp	olive oil	60 mL

Combine the first 5 ingredients. Beat together the egg white and buttermilk. Dip chicken into egg mixture and then into oat bran mixture. Press coating firmly onto chicken. Let stand 10 minutes, or refrigerate several hours, before cooking as coating will adhere better. Heat half the oil in a large skillet over medium heat. Add chicken and cook 4 minutes. Turn and add remaining oil. Cook until chicken feels springy when pressed and is no longer pink in the centre.
Serves 6.

Chicken in Wine Sauce

3		chicken breasts, skinned, boned and halved	3
1	cup	plain yogurt	250 mL
3	Tbsp	flour	45 mL
½	cup	white wine	125 mL
1		can (10oz/284mL) mushroom soup	1
½	cup	slivered almonds	125 mL
2	Tbsp	chopped pimiento	30 mL
1	tsp	paprika	5 mL

Preheat oven to 325°F (160°C).
Roll chicken pieces and place in a shallow baking dish. Combine flour with ¼ cup (50mL) yogurt, mixing until smooth. Add remaining yogurt, wine and soup and pour over chicken. Sprinkle with remaining ingredients.
Bake for 1½ hours.
Serves 6.

Curried Orange Chicken

3	lb	chicken, cut up	1.5 kg
2	Tbsp	butter	30 mL
½	cup	chopped onion	125 mL
½	cup	chopped celery	125 mL
1		clove garlic, minced	1
1	tsp	tumeric	5 mL
1	tsp	ground coriander	5 mL
½	tsp	fennel seeds	2 mL
½	tsp	salt	2 mL
¼	tsp	ground ginger	1 mL
¼	tsp	cumin	1 mL
⅛	tsp	cayenne	.5 mL
1	Tbsp	flour	15 mL
½	cup	orange juice	125 mL
½	cup	water	125 mL
1	cup	chopped peeled tomatoes	250 mL
1		green pepper, cut in strips	1
2	cups	fresh orange sections	500 mL
		cooked rice	
		toasted coconut	
		golden raisins	

Melt butter in a large skillet and add chicken pieces and brown on all sides. Remove chicken. Add onions, celery, garlic and spices. Cook until vegetables are crisp tender. Blend in flour. Stir in orange juice and water and bring to a boil, stirring constantly. Add chicken, tomatoes and peppers. Cover and simmer 30 minutes or until chicken is tender. Stir in orange sections and heat.
Serve with rice, sprinkle with coconut and raisins.
Serves 4.

Curry Honey Chicken

4		chicken breast halves, boned and skinned	4
¾	tsp	minced fresh ginger	3 mL
½	tsp	salt	2 mL
½	tsp	pepper	2 mL
1		medium onion, thinly sliced	1
1		lemon, thinly sliced	1
¾	cup	dry white wine	175 mL
¼	cup	honey	50 mL
1	Tbsp	curry powder	15 mL

Preheat oven to 400°F (200°C).
Combine ginger, salt and pepper and rub into chicken. Layer onion in a greased 1 qt (1L) baking dish. Top with chicken then lemon slices. Pour wine over.
Bake for 50 minutes. During the last 20 minutes baste with honey and curry mixture. Serve with rice.
Serves 4.

Parmesan Yogurt Chicken

4		whole chicken breasts, halved boned and skinned	4
2	Tbsp	lemon juice	30 mL
¼	tsp	cayenne pepper	1 mL
1	cup	plain yogurt	250 mL
2	Tbsp	instant blending flour	30 mL
¼	cup	light mayonnaise	50 mL
2	Tbsp	Dijon mustard	30 mL
½	tsp	thyme	2 mL
¼	tsp	Worcestershire sauce	1 mL
¼	cup	minced green onion	50 mL
2	Tbsp	grated parmesan cheese paprika additional parmesan cheese chopped green onion	30 mL

Preheat oven to 350°F (180°C).
Arrange chicken in a lightly oiled baking dish. Drizzle with lemon juice and sprinkle with cayenne pepper. Mix together the yogurt and flour. Stir in the next 6 ingredients and spread over the chicken. Sprinkle with paprika and parmesan cheese.
Bake for 1 hour.
Sprinkle with chopped green onion before serving.
Serves 6-8.

Grilled Turkey Steaks

Juicy and flavourful.

2		turkey steaks, at least ½" (1.5cm) thick	2
1	Tbsp	Dijon mustard	15 mL
1	tsp	fresh tarragon	5 mL
		freshly ground pepper	

Blanch the steaks in boiling water for 2 minutes. Remove and pat dry. Generously rub steaks all over with mustard. Sprinkle with tarragon and pepper.
Grill 5-6" (13-15cm) from high heat about 5 minutes per side. Do not overcook.
Serves 2.

Easy Maui Ribs

A taste of Hawaii in your own backyard.

2	lb	"Maui" cut beef shortribs	1 kg
½	cup	teriyaki sauce	125 mL
½	cup	soy sauce	125 mL
½	cup	brown sugar	125 mL
½		can (10oz/284mL) beef consommé	½
¼	cup	sherry	50 mL
1	tsp	grated fresh ginger	5 mL
1	tsp	sesame oil	5 mL
4-6		cloves garlic, minced	4-6

Place ribs in a ziplock plastic bag or leak-proof marinating container. Combine the remaining ingredients and add to the bag. Expel air and seal. Refrigerate 4-5 days turning container over daily. Barbecue to rare or medium. Enjoy!
Serves 4.

Beef Fantastic

An elegant entrée for a special occasion.

3	lb	beef tenderloin	1.5 kg
1½	Tbsp	butter	22 mL
2	tsp	dry mustard	10 mL
		salt and pepper	
4		shallots, chopped	4
1	cup	sliced mushrooms	250 mL
¼	cup	butter	50 mL
½	cup	dry red wine	125 mL
½	cup	beef consommé	125 mL
1	tsp	cornstarch	5 mL
½	tsp	lemon juice	2 mL

Preheat oven to 300°F (150°C).

Dry meat with a paper towel. Combine butter and mustard to form a paste and spread over all surfaces of the meat. Sprinkle with salt and pepper and place on a rack in a roasting pan.

Bake for 1 hour.

Sauté onions and mushrooms in butter until mushrooms begin to brown. Add wine and cook until reduced by half. Add consommé that has been mixed with cornstarch and simmer until thickened. Add lemon juice and pour over cooked filet.

Serves 6-8.

Hearty Beef Stew

This robust stew can be made several days in advance.

2	lb	stew meat	1 kg
⅓	cup	flour	75 mL
2	Tbsp	oil	30 mL
1		bottle dry red wine	1
1		large onion, sliced	1
2		cloves garlic, minced	2
2	Tbsp	Worcestershire sauce	30 mL
1	tsp	salt	5 mL
½	tsp	thyme	2 mL
¼	tsp	pepper	1 mL
2		bay leaves	2
½	lb	small mushrooms	250 g
2		celery stalks, sliced	2
4		carrots, sliced	4
4		potatoes, cut in chunks	4
2	Tbsp	flour	30 mL
¼	cup	water	50 mL

Dredge meat in flour and brown in oil in a dutch oven. Add wine, onion and garlic. Cover and simmer for 1½ hours. Cool and refrigerate for at least 1-2 days to develop flavours. Skim off fat. Add the next 5 ingredients and simmer for 30 minutes. Add the vegetables and cook an additional 30-40 minutes until tender. Remove bay leaves. Combine flour and water, stirring until smooth, and stir into stew. Cook and stir until thickened.
Serves 6.

Beef Vindaloo

2	lb	round steak	1	kg
2	Tbsp	ground coriander	30	mL
2	tsp	ground tumeric	10	mL
2	tsp	dry mustard	10	mL
2	tsp	chili powder	10	mL
2	tsp	cayenne pepper	10	mL
1	tsp	ground cumin	5	mL
½	tsp	pepper	2	mL
½	tsp	ground ginger	2	mL
½	cup	red wine vinegar	125	mL
3		medium onions, sliced	3	
5		hot jalapeño peppers, minced	5	
6		cloves garlic, minced	6	
1		slice (3"/7.5cm) gingerroot	1	
¼	cup	olive oil	50	mL

Cut beef into 1" (2.5cm) cubes and set aside. Combine the next 8 ingredients. Add the vinegar and stir to make a paste. Set aside. Sauté the next 4 ingredients in the oil for 3 minutes. Add the paste and sauté for a further 3 minutes. Transfer to a casserole, add beef and cover.
Bake for 2-2½ hours.
Serve with boiled rice and garnish with tomato wedges, coconut, sliced bananas, *etc.*
Serves 6.

Sweet and Sour Ribs

Tender and tasty!

2-4	lb	lean back pork ribs garlic salt and pepper to taste	1-2 kg

Preheat broiler.
Season ribs and broil on each side until brown and crisp. Let cool then cut into strips. Place ribs in a casserole and cover with sauce.
Reduce oven temperature to 325°F(160°C).
Bake covered for 2 hours.

Sauce

1⅓	cups	ketchup	325 mL
½	cup	sugar	125 mL
¼	cup	vinegar	50 mL
¼	cup	water	50 mL
1	Tbsp	cornstarch	15 mL
1	Tbsp	soy sauce	15 mL

Combine all ingredients in a medium saucepan. Bring to a boil over medium heat to thicken. Pour over ribs.
Serves 4-6.

Pork Tenderloin

1	lb	pork tenderloin, sliced and frenched	500 g
3	Tbsp	sherry	45 mL
½	tsp	marjoram	2 mL
½	tsp	pepper	2 mL
¾	cup	chopped onion	175 mL
¾	cup	chopped celery	175 mL
3	Tbsp	white wine	45 mL
6	oz	mushrooms, sliced	170 g
1	tsp	vegetable oil	5 mL
1		can (10oz/284mL) mushroom soup	1
⅓	cup	chopped toasted almonds	75 mL
3		green onions, chopped	3

Preheat oven to 275°F (140°C).
Marinate the first 4 ingredients in a casserole for 20 minutes at room temperature or 4 hours in the refrigerator. Cook the onion and celery in the wine for 5 minutes, or microwave for 2 minutes. Add to pork. Combine remaining ingredients and spread over meat mixture. Cover.
Bake for 2½-3 hours.
Serves 4.

Party Pork Loin

5-6	lb	boneless pork loin	2½-3 kg
¾	cup	Dijon mustard	175 mL
¼	cup	olive oil	50 mL
2	Tbsp	white wine	30 mL
3		cloves garlic, minced	3
⅓	cup	rosemary	75 mL

Preheat oven to 325°F (160°C).
Stir together the mustard, oil, wine and garlic. Untie roast and spread mixture thickly inside. Sprinkle generously with rosemary. Retie roast and spread remaining mixture over the entire outside. Sprinkle with rosemary. Refrigerate several hours.
Bake for 2½ hours.
Serves 10-12.

Minted Lamb Chops

8		loin lamb chops 1" (2.5cm) thick	8
4	Tbsp	mint jelly	60 mL
4	tsp	dry mustard	20 mL
1	Tbsp	sage	15 mL
2		cloves garlic, minced	2
½	tsp	ground fresh pepper	2 mL

Remove the fat from outside of the lamb. Combine the remaining ingredients and microwave on medium for 1 minute. Cool until thickened. Spread onto chops. This may be done just before cooking or several hours in advance. Barbecue or broil until done to your liking. Serve with mint jelly.
Serves 4.

Super Sizzle Ham

2		ham steaks ¾" (2cm) thick	2
1½	cups	orange juice	375 mL
½	cup	vinegar	125 mL
½	cup	brown sugar	125 mL
2	Tbsp	ground cloves	30 mL
2	Tbsp	brandy	30 mL
1	Tbsp	dry mustard	15 mL
1	Tbsp	ground ginger	15 mL

Place ham steaks in a container for marinating. Combine remaining ingredients and pour over ham. Marinate 2-3 hours, turning several times.

Barbeque or grill just long enough to heat through.

Serves 6-8.

Kate's Lazom Zipstew

Comes from Jurgen Gothe, host of Discdrive heard across Canada on CBC Stereo weekday afternoons.

	few slices lean bacon, diced	
2	large cloves garlic, chopped	2
4-5	firm shallots, chopped	4-5
1	lean lamb leg or roast, cubed	1
	coarse black pepper	
	beef or chicken stock	
	red or white wine, depending on the stock	
2	small zucchini	2
½ cup	crumbly dry sun dried tomatoes	125 mL
	fresh or canned oyster mushrooms	
	fresh thyme and parsley	
1	avocado, peeled and cubed	1
	juice of 1 lemon	

Sauté bacon until most of the fat is removed; reserve. Sauté garlic and shallots in a little of the fat; reserve. Brown lamb, sprinkle with pepper, add stock and appropriate wine. Sprinkle with tomatoes and canned oyster mushrooms (if using fresh add later with the zucchini). Add thyme and parsley and cook over medium high heat until a little of the liquid is reduced. Cover and simmer 15-20 minutes until the lamb is the tenderness you like. Do not overcook or it will be rubbery. Sprinkle avocado with lemon juice and reserve. Five minutes before the stew is cooked add the zucchini and fresh oyster mushrooms which have been cut in pieces. When cooked, remove from heat and stir in avocado and lemon juice.
Serve in big heated bowls with pepper focaccia bread or Portuguese buns.
Note: Jurgen Gothe explains Lazom as his acronym for the main ingredients: lamb, avocado, zucchini and oyster mushrooms, and zipstew is his term for a fast one that tastes like you've spent 2½ days on it.

Excellent Veal Deal

Pork or turkey cutlets may be substituted with equally excellent results.

4-6		lean veal chops	4-6
3	Tbsp	flour	45 mL
1	tsp	vegetable oil	5 mL
½		can (10oz/284mL) beef bouillon	½
½	cup	low fat plain yogurt	125 mL
¼	cup	dry sherry	50 mL
1		lemon, juice and grated rind	1
1	Tbsp	flour	15 mL
⅛	tsp	thyme	.5 mL
1	cup	sliced mushrooms, sautéed (optional)	250 mL

Dredge meat in flour then brown in oil in a heavy skillet. Remove meat and add the next 6 ingredients to the pan, stirring until smooth. Cook and stir over low heat until thick. Return meat to sauce, cover and cook over low heat for 30 minutes. Add mushrooms and serve.
Serves 4-6.

Seafood Linguine

¼	lb	mushrooms, sliced	125 g
2		cloves garlic, minced	2
1	Tbsp	butter	15 mL
½	cup	dry white wine	125 mL
1		can (10oz/284mL) baby clams with liquid	1
1	Tbsp	lemon juice	15 mL
½	tsp	oregano	2 mL
½	tsp	Italian herbs	2 mL
¼	tsp	nutmeg	1 mL
		dash cayenne pepper	
6	oz	cream cheese, cut in small pieces	170 g
6	oz	shrimp	170 g
6	oz	crab or cooked fish	170 g
2		medium tomatoes, chopped	2
¼	cup	chopped parsley	50 mL
1	lb	fresh linguine, cooked	500 g
¼	cup	parmesan cheese	50 mL

In a skillet sauté mushrooms and garlic in butter. Add the next 7 ingredients and heat. Add the cheese stirring until melted, but do not boil. Stir in the next 4 ingredients and heat through. Pour sauce over linguine and toss to coat. Sprinkle with parmesan.
Serves 6.

Vegetables and Side Dishes

Sky High Vegetable Pie

1		pkg Stove Top Stuffing mix	1
1		egg, lightly beaten	1
1		onion, chopped	1
1		clove garlic, minced	1
1	Tbsp	butter	15 mL
2		pkg (10oz/280g) frozen chopped spinach, thawed and well drained	2
8	oz	mozzarella cheese, grated	250 g
½		red pepper, cut in strips	½
4		eggs, lightly beaten	4
2		tomatoes, sliced	2

Preheat oven to 400°F (200°C).
Prepare stuffing according to package directions. Add egg and mix. Press into an 8" (20cm) spring form pan to form crust. Sauté the next 3 ingredients until tender. Remove from heat and add spinach. Sprinkle half the cheese over crust, top with half the spinach then the red pepper. Sprinkle with remaining cheese then spinach. Pour eggs over top.
Bake for 40-45 minutes until set. During the last 10 minutes layer the tomatoes over the top.
Note: After removing from oven let dish set for 10 minutes before removing pan sides and serving.
Serves 8.

Green Beans Oriental

1½	lb	green beans, whole or sliced	750 g
1	cup	sliced fresh mushrooms	250 mL
¼	cup	chopped onion	50 mL
1	Tbsp	butter	15 mL
2	cups	bean sprouts	500 mL
1		can (8oz/227mL) water chestnuts, drained and sliced	1
1		can (10oz/284mL) mushroom soup	1
⅓		soup can milk	⅓
½	cup	grated old cheddar cheese	125 mL
1		can (3oz/85g) french fried onions	1

Cook beans until barely crisp tender. Drain and set aside. Sauté mushrooms and onion in butter 3-4 minutes. Remove from heat and stir in bean sprouts and water chestnuts. Combine soup and milk. Layer half the beans in a shallow 2 qt (2L) casserole. Top with half the mushroom sprout mixture and half the soup. Repeat. Sprinkle cheese over top. Sprinkle onions over top the last 5 minutes of baking.
Bake for 25 minutes or until hot and bubbly. Do not overcook.
Serves 8.

Beans with Lime Basil Butter

2	lb	sliced green beans	1 kg
¼	cup	butter, melted	50 mL
2	Tbsp	chopped fresh basil	30 mL
1	Tbsp	lime juice	15 mL
¼	tsp	grated lime rind	1 mL
¼	cup	pine nuts, toasted	50 mL

Cook green beans until crisp tender. Combine the next 4 ingredients
and pour over beans. Sprinkle with nuts and serve.
Serves 8.

Walnut Sugar Peas

½	lb	sugar snap peas	250 g
¼	cup	apple juice	50 mL
2	Tbsp	water	30 mL
2	tsp	walnut oil	10 mL
1	tsp	cornstarch	5 mL
		pepper to taste	
2	Tbsp	broken walnuts	30 mL
½		apple, peeled, cored and sliced in thin julienne	½

Cook peas in boiling water until crisp tender, 1-2 minutes. Drain.
Combine the next 5 ingredients in a bowl and microwave on high for
2 minutes until thick, stirring twice. Pour over peas and toss to coat.
Sprinkle with nuts and apple.
Serves 4.

Veggie Bundles

An interesting way to serve vegetables.

6		carrots, cut in 5" (13cm) julienne strips	6
4		parnips, cut in 5" (13cm) julienne strips	4
3		leeks, cut in 5" (13cm) strips	3
2		bunches green onions, white ends cut off and reserved	2
3	Tbsp	butter	45 mL
2		cloves garlic, crushed white part of green onions, chopped	2
1	tsp	tarragon chopped fresh dill to taste	5 mL

Blanch carrots for 1½ minutes, parsnips for 1 minute, leeks for 30 seconds, and green onion stems for 5 seconds. To assemble each bundle, securely tie softened green onion around 6 carrot strips, 3 parsnip strips, 2 white leek pieces and 2 green leek pieces. Sauté remaining ingredients in butter. Roll bundles in this mixture to coat, arrange in serving dish and warm in microwave just before serving. Garnish with fresh dill.
Serves 8.

Vegetable Medley

2	tsp	olive oil	10 mL
1		small onion, chopped	1
2	cups	broccoli florets	500 mL
2	cups	fresh snow peas	500 mL
2	cups	bean sprouts	500 mL
1		cube chicken bouillon, dissolved in	1
½	cup	boiling water	125 mL
2	Tbsp	light soy sauce	30 mL

Heat oil in a frying pan or wok. Add the onion and broccoli and stir fry for 2 minutes. Add the snow peas and stir. Lay bean sprouts on top. Pour bouillon and soy sauce over vegetables. Cover and simmer 2-3 minutes. Do not overcook.
Serves 6.

Tomato Treat

1		can (28oz/750mL) tomatoes	1
1		can (5½oz/156mL) tomato paste	1
2	cups	crustless bread cubes	500 mL
2	Tbsp	brown sugar	30 mL
½	tsp	freshly ground pepper	2 mL
½	tsp	dried basil	2 mL
½	tsp	Italian seasoning	2 mL
1	Tbsp	butter	15 mL

Preheat oven to 350°F (180°C).
Combine the first 7 ingredients and pour into a lightly oiled deep casserole dish. Dot with butter.
Bake for 1 hour.
Serves 7.

Make Ahead Vegetable Medley

3		large carrots, diagonally sliced ¼"(.5cm) thick	3
1½	lb	broccoli (about 8 cups/2L), trimmed	750 g
1		medium cauliflower	1

Sauce

¼	cup	butter	50 mL
¼	cup	flour	50 mL
2¾	cups	milk	675 mL
1½	cups	grated cheddar cheese	375 mL
2	Tbsp	chopped parsley	30 mL
1	Tbsp	Dijon mustard	15 mL

Topping

1	cup	breadcrumbs	250 mL
½	cup	grated parmesan cheese	125 mL
2	Tbsp	melted butter	30 mL

Preheat oven to 325°F (160°C).
Cook carrots until crisp tender. Cut broccoli tops, peeled stems and cauliflower into serving size pieces and blanch in a pot of boiling water for 2 minutes. Drain and plunge into ice water to cool. Drain and turn into a shallow 3 qt (3L) casserole.

Sauce
Melt butter in a pan over medium heat, stir in flour and cook a few seconds. Stir in milk and cook until thickened and smooth, stirring constantly. Add remaining sauce ingredients and stir until cheese melts. Pour over vegetables, cover and refrigerate until ready to bake.

Topping
Combine topping ingredients and sprinkle over casserole just before baking.
Bake covered for 45-50 minutes until hot and bubbly.
Serves 10.

Saucy Stir Fried Vegetables

Soup mix creates the sauce in this recipe.

1		pouch chicken noodle supreme soup mix	1
1	cup	water	250 mL
1	Tbsp	soy sauce	15 mL
1	tsp	sugar	5 mL
1	tsp	vegetable oil	5 mL
1½	cups	snow peas, halved	375 mL
1	cup	sliced mushrooms	250 mL
½	cup	red pepper strips	125 mL
1		medium zucchini, cubed	1
2		green onions, diagonally sliced	2
½	cup	slivered almonds	125 mL

 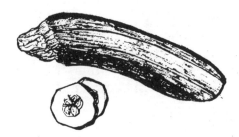

Combine the first 4 ingredients in a small saucepan. Bring to a boil, reduce heat, cover and simmer for 7 minutes. In a large skillet over medium high heat stir-fry the remaining ingredients in the oil until crisp tender, about 3 minutes. Pour soup mixture over, stirring to combine.
Serves 4.

Spinach Casserole

3		eggs	3
2	Tbsp	flour	30 mL
1		pkg (10oz/300g) frozen chopped spinach, cooked and drained	1
6	oz	cheddar cheese, grated	170 g
4	oz	cottage cheese	125 g
⅛	tsp	freshly ground pepper	.5 mL
2	Tbsp	butter	30 mL

Preheat oven to 350°F (180°C).

Beat eggs and flour until smooth. Stir in spinach. Add the next 3 ingredients mixing thoroughly. Melt butter in a 9"(22cm) square baking dish, and pour mixture in.

Bake for 30 minutes or until set. The recipe doubled takes about 45 minutes.

Let stand for 10 minutes before cutting.

Note: This recipe can be assembled the day before and baked before serving.

Serves 6.

Broccoli Casserole

1	lb	broccoli florets in bite size pieces	500 g
½		onion, chopped	½
2	cups	cottage cheese	500 mL
1	cup	grated cheddar cheese	250 mL
3	Tbsp	melted butter	45 mL
3	Tbsp	flour	45 mL
3		eggs	3
½	tsp	ground pepper	2 mL
½	tsp	garlic powder	2 mL
½	tsp	dried basil	2 mL

Preheat oven to 350°F (180°C).
Arrange broccoli and onion in an oiled 7x11" (18x28cm) baking dish.
Combine remaining ingredients and spoon over broccoli.
Bake for 45 minutes or until top is golden brown.
Serves 6-8.

Potatoes Almondine

4		medium potatoes, cooked and mashed	4
1½	cups	cottage cheese	375 mL
¼	cup	yogurt	50 mL
2	Tbsp	chopped green onion	30 mL
1	tsp	salt	5 mL
¼	tsp	pepper	1 mL
¼	cup	sliced almonds	50 mL
2	Tbsp	melted butter	30 mL

Preheat oven to 350°F (180°C).
Combine the first 6 ingredients and beat until smooth. Place in a shallow greased casserole, brush with butter, sprinkle with almonds.
Bake for 30 minutes.
Serves 6.

Beets in Currant Sauce

1	lb	cooked whole baby beets or sliced beets	500 g
½	cup	water	125 mL
½	cup	red currant jelly	125 mL
2	Tbsp	orange juice	30 mL
⅛	tsp	nutmeg	.5 mL

Combine the sauce ingredients and cook until slightly thickened. Pour over the hot beets. Canned beets may be used in place of fresh. Serves 4.

Impossible Broccoli Pie

Super easy and super good!

1		pkg (10oz/280g) frozen or fresh chopped broccoli	1
1	cup	grated medium cheddar cheese	250 mL
¼	cup	finely chopped onion	50 mL
2		eggs	2
¾	cup	milk	175 mL
½	cup	tea biscuit mix (recipe page 136) salt, pepper and celery seed to taste	125 mL

Preheat oven to 400°F (200°C).
Spread broccoli over bottom of a 9" (22cm) pie plate. Sprinkle with onion and then with cheese. Place remaining ingredients into a blender or food processor and blend until smooth. Pour over cheese. Bake for 25-35 minutes or until set. Cut into wedges.
Serves 6-8.

Broccoli and Tomatoes

Zesty and colourful.

1		large bunch broccoli, trimmed and peeled	1
¼	cup	olive oil	50 mL
¼	tsp	dried red pepper flakes	1 mL
3		cloves garlic, minced	3
¾	cup	pine nuts	175 mL
4		large tomatoes, coarsely chopped	4
1	Tbsp	chopped parsley	15 mL
½	tsp	pepper	2 mL

Cut broccoli tops into florets and slice stems. Blanch in boiling water for 1 minute. Drain. Heat oil in skillet, add pepper flakes and stir. Add garlic and nuts and sauté until nuts just begin to colour. Add broccoli and sauté until just crisp tender. Add tomatoes and heat. Sprinkle parsley and pepper over.
Serves 8.

Apricot Glazed Carrots

2	lb	carrots, cut on the diagonal	1 kg
3	Tbsp	butter or margarine	45 mL
⅓	cup	apricot preserves or jam	75 mL
2	tsp	lemon juice	10 mL
1	tsp	grated orange peel	5 mL
¼	tsp	nutmeg	1 mL
⅛	tsp	pepper	.5 mL

Cook carrots until crisp tender. Drain. Melt butter in saucepan and add remaining ingredients, stirring until well blended. Add carrots and toss until well coated.
Serves 8-10.

Cauliflower Tasties

¼	cup	grated parmesan cheese	50 mL
¼	cup	dry breadcrumbs	50 mL
1	tsp	tarragon	5 mL
1	tsp	paprika	5 mL
½	tsp	salt	2 mL
		dash of pepper	
1		small cauliflower, cut in small florets	1
⅓	cup	butter, melted	75 mL

Preheat oven to 325°F (160°C).
Combine the first 6 ingredients in a plastic bag. Dip the cauliflower pieces in butter and drop into the bag. Shake to coat. Arrange cauliflower in a single layer in a 7x11" (18x28cm) baking dish.
Bake for 10-12 minutes or microwave on a paper towel for 4-5 minutes until crisp tender.
Serves 6.

Braised Belgian Endive

Equally good with hearts of romaine lettuce.

6		medium Belgian endives	6
1	Tbsp	white wine	15 mL
1½	tsp	vegetable oil	7 mL
1	tsp	sugar	5 mL
½	tsp	salt	2 mL
		freshly ground pepper	
½	cup	water	125 mL

Place endive in a single layer in a stainless steel or glass saucepan. Sprinkle with the next 5 ingredients. Add water. Cover pan and bring to a boil. Reduce heat and simmer 15-20 minutes depending on endive size. Uncover and increase heat, boil until liquid is reduced to 3 Tbsp (45mL). Serve hot, drizzled with reduced cooking liquid. Serves 6.

Rice with Vermicelli

1	cup	long grain rice	250 mL
⅓	cup	fine vermicelli, broken	75 mL
2	tsp	butter	10 mL
2	cups	boiling chicken broth or water	500 mL
¼	cup	toasted pine nuts (optional)	50 mL

Rinse rice and drain. Melt butter in a saucepan and sauté vermicelli over medium heat until golden brown. Add rice and sauté gently for 1-2 minutes. Add boiling broth and bring rice mixture to a boil. Lower heat to medium and boil until most of the water is absorbed. Cover pan tightly and leave on low heat for 10 minutes until completely dry. Remove from heat and let stand, covered, for 10 minutes. Garnish with pine nuts.
Serves 4.

Mediterranean Couscous

Serve hot as a side dish or cold as a salad.

1	cup	chicken broth	250 mL
1	tsp	dried basil	5 mL
¼	tsp	ground celery seed	1 mL
¼	tsp	pepper	1 mL
¾	cup	couscous	175 mL
1		tomato, chopped	1
2		green onions, chopped	2
2	Tbsp	chopped green pepper	30 mL
2	tsp	chopped parsley	10 mL
2	tsp	balsamic vinegar	10 mL
2	tsp	olive oil	10 mL

Bring the first 4 ingredients to a boil in a medium saucepan. Stir in couscous, cover, and remove from heat. Let stand 5 minutes. Combine remaining ingredients, heat and stir into couscous. Serves 6.

Orzo with Parmesan & Basil

Rice shaped pasta with the rich flavour of parmesan cheese.

2	Tbsp	butter or margarine	30 mL
1½	cups	orzo	375 mL
3	cups	chicken stock	750 mL
½	cup	grated parmesan cheese	125 mL
⅓	cup	chopped fresh basil	75 mL
1	Tbsp	chopped parsley	15 mL
¼	tsp	pepper	1 mL
		pinch of nutmeg	

Melt butter in a heavy skillet and sauté orzo 2-3 minutes. Add stock, cover and simmer 20 minutes until water is absorbed and orzo is tender. Remove from heat and stir in remaining ingredients. Serves 6.

Vegetable Pulao

A great vegetarian dish or serve with Honey-Lemon Chicken on page 78 in *Fast & Fantastic*.

3	Tbsp	vegetable oil	45 mL
¼	cup	diced onion	50 mL
1	tsp	cumin seeds	5 mL
1	tsp	cinnamon	5 mL
6		whole cloves	6
6		peppercorns	6
3		bay leaves	3
1½	cups	Basmati rice	375 mL
3	cups	water	750 mL
¾	cups	chopped carrots	175 mL
¼	cup	sultana raisins	50 mL
1	tsp	salt	5 mL
1	tsp	garam masala (page 187)	5 mL
¼	tsp	ground tumeric	1 mL
¼	tsp	red chili powder	1 mL
¼	tsp	ground cardamom	1 mL
¾	cup	frozen peas	175 mL
½	cup	cashew nuts	125 mL

Sauté the first 7 ingredients in a large saucepan on medium heat until onion is soft. Add rice and sauté 3-4 minutes. Add remaining ingredients, except peas and nuts, cover and cook for approximately 20 minutes on medium heat. Add the peas and cashews the last 5 minutes of cooking.
Serves 6.

Casual

Brunch Eggs

½	lb	bacon, cooked crisp, drained and chopped (optional)	250 g
1		can (10oz/284mL) mushroom soup	1
¼	cup	sherry	50 mL
18		eggs	18
2	Tbsp	milk	30 mL
1	tsp	chopped parsley	5 mL
½	tsp	dried dill	2 mL
		pepper to taste	
1	Tbsp	vegetable oil	15 mL
¼	lb	sliced mushrooms	125 g
¼	cup	chopped green onions	50 mL
1½	cups	shredded Monterey Jack cheese	375 mL
1½	cups	shredded cheddar cheese	375 mL
		paprika	

Preheat oven to 300°F (150°C).
Combine soup and sherry. Beat together the next 5 ingredients.
Sauté mushrooms and onions in oil. Add egg mixture and cook until barely set. Add bacon if desired. Spoon half the egg mixture into a deep 9x13" (22x34cm) greased baking dish. Cover with half the soup mixture and half the cheeses. Repeat and sprinkle with paprika.
Bake uncovered for about 1 hour.
Note: For those on a low cholesterol diet, egg beaters, skim milk and low fat cheeses may be substituted.
Serves 12.

Chili Egg Soufflé

A great brunch dish that also reheats well.

10		eggs	10
½	cup	flour	125 mL
1	tsp	baking powder	5 mL
		dash of salt	
1	lb	Jack cheese, grated	500 g
2	cups	2% cottage cheese	500 mL
½	cup	butter, melted	125 mL
1		can (7oz/213mL) chopped green chilies	1

Preheat oven to 350°F (180°C).
Beat eggs until light and lemon coloured. Blend in the next 3 ingredients. Add the remaining ingredients and mix thoroughly.
Pour into a greased 9x13" (22 x 34 cm) baking dish.
Bake for 40-45 minutes until edges are set and lightly browned.
Cut in squares.
Serves 8.

Omelette Sauce

½	lb	mushrooms, sliced	250 g
½		onion, diced	½
½		green pepper, diced	½
1		can (14oz/398mL) tomatoes	1
3	Tbsp	ketchup	45 mL
1½	Tbsp	Worcestershire sauce	22 mL
10		drops Tabasco sauce	10
		salt and pepper to taste	

In medium saucepan sauté the first 3 ingredients in oil until browned. Add tomatoes and simmer until soft. Add remaining ingredients, simmering gently.
Makes enough sauce for 6 individual omelettes.

Heavenly Seafood Rolls

Super luncheon or casual supper dish.

Filling

½		onion, chopped	½
1		stalk celery, chopped	1
¼		green pepper, grated	¼
1	Tbsp	butter	15 mL
1		can (7.5oz/213g) crab or salmon	1
½	cup	grated cheddar cheese	125 mL
¼	cup	mayonnaise	50 mL
		fish seasoning (optional)	
⅛	tsp	pepper	.5 mL

Biscuit Dough

2	cups	flour	500 mL
4	tsp	baking powder	20 mL
1	Tbsp	sugar	15 mL
½	cup	vegetable shortening or margarine	125 mL
½	cup	grated cheddar cheese	125 mL
⅔	cup	skim milk	150 mL
1		egg, beaten	1

Sauce

10		mushrooms, sliced	10
1	Tbsp	butter	15 mL
1		can (10oz/284mL) mushroom soup	1
½	cup	skim milk	125 mL
2	tsp	Worcestershire sauce	10 mL
½	tsp	prepared mustard	2 mL

Preheat oven to 400°F (200°C).
Sauté the first 3 ingredients in butter for 3-5 minutes. Remove from heat and stir in the remaining filling ingredients and set aside.
To prepare biscuit dough, sift dry ingredients together into a bowl.

Cut in shortening and add cheese. Stir in milk and egg with a fork. Turn dough out onto a floured board and knead several times. Roll into a 12" (30cm) square. Spread on filling and roll up jelly roll style, sealing bottom edge with water. Cut into 12 pinwheels. Place in 2 greased pie plates cut side up.
Bake for 30 minutes.
While baking prepare sauce. Gently sauté mushrooms in butter. Add remaining ingredients and heat through. Serve over hot rolls.
Serves 6.

Crispy Tuna Casserole

A family favourite that's quick to assemble.

1		can (6.5oz/184g) tuna, drained and broken into small chunks	1
½	lb	mushrooms, sliced	250 g
1	cup	thinly sliced celery	250 mL
1	cup	chopped onion	250 mL
1	Tbsp	vegetable oil	15 mL
1		can (10oz/284mL) mushroom soup	1
1	Tbsp	soy sauce	15 mL
⅛	tsp	Tabasco sauce	.5 mL
½	cup	sliced water chestnuts	125 mL
5	cups	chow mein noodles	1.25 L

Preheat oven to 375°F (190°C).
Place tuna in a 1½ qt (1.5L) casserole dish. Sauté the next 3 ingredients in oil for 3 minutes. Mix into tuna. Combine soup, soy sauce and Tabasco and add with the remaining ingredients, tossing to combine.
Bake for 30 minutes.
Serves 4-5.

Apricot Shrimp Curry

The magic of the microwave makes this delicious dish super quick.

½	cup	slivered almonds	125 mL
2	Tbsp	mango chutney	30 mL
1	Tbsp	butter	15 mL
2		cloves garlic, minced	2
2	tsp	curry powder	10 mL
2	tsp	grated fresh ginger	10 mL
6		apricots, quartered	6
¾	cup	celery in ¼" (.5cm) slices	175 mL
¾	lb	shrimp	375 g
¼	cup	plain yogurt	50 mL
2	tsp	lime juice	10 mL

Cook almonds in microwave at high for 4-5 minutes, stirring occasionally. Combine the next 5 ingredients in a 2½ qt (2.5L) casserole. Microwave for 1½ minutes, covered. Add apricots and celery and cook for 3 minutes. Stir in almonds and shrimp. Cover and cook for 1 minute more. Stir in yogurt and lime juice.
Serves 4-6.

Scallops in White Wine

¼	lb	mushrooms sliced	125 g
2		small zucchini, sliced ¼" (1cm) thick	2
2		green onions, chopped	2
2	tsp	vegetable oil	10 mL
1		large tomato, chopped	1
1		clove garlic, minced	1
2	Tbsp	white wine	30 mL
⅛	tsp	basil	.5 mL
⅛	tsp	oregano	.5 mL
½	lb	scallops, halved if large	250 g
2	Tbsp	breadcrumbs	30 mL
1	tsp	parmesan cheese	5 mL

Preheat broiler.
Sauté the first 3 ingredients in oil, over medium heat, for 2 minutes.
Add the next 5 ingredients and cook 2 minutes. Add scallops, cover and simmer until scallops are just cooked, 1-2 minutes. Place mixture in 4 small ovenproof ramekins or 1 casserole dish. Sprinkle with combined crumbs and parmesan.
Broil 1-2 minutes.
Serves 4 as an appetizer or 2 as an entrée.

Mexican Strata

4	cups	tortilla chips	1 L
2	cups	shredded Monterey Jack cheese	500 mL
6		eggs	6
2½	cups	milk	625 mL
1		can (4oz/114mL) chopped green chilies, drained	1
½	cup	chopped onion	125 mL
3	Tbsp	ketchup	45 mL
½	tsp	salt	2 mL
¼	tsp	Tabasco sauce	1 mL

Preheat oven to 325°F (160°C).
Break tortillas and sprinkle in a greased 9x11" (22x28cm) pan.
Sprinkle cheese over. Beat eggs and milk together, mix in remaining
ingredients and pour over cheese. Cover and refrigerate several
hours or overnight.
Bake for 50-55 minutes until set.
Serves 6-8.

Chicken Sparta

This is a super dish for a brunch or luncheon.

¾	lb	mushrooms, sliced	375	g
2	Tbsp	finely chopped onion	30	mL
2	Tbsp	butter or margarine	30	mL
9		slices of bread, crusts removed	9	
4	cups	diced cooked chicken	1	L
1		can (8oz/227mL) sliced water chestnuts, drained	1	
½	lb	sharp cheddar cheese, sliced	250	g
4		eggs	4	
2	cups	milk	500	mL
1		can (10oz/284mL) mushroom soup	1	
1		can (10oz/284mL) celery soup (do not substitute)	1	
1	cup	buttered breadcrumbs	250	mL

Preheat oven to 350°F (180°C).
Sauté mushrooms and onion in butter for 3-4 minutes. Line a greased 11x13" (28x34cm) deep baking dish with bread. Top with chicken, then water chestnuts and mushrooms. Add cheese slices. Beat eggs and milk and pour over top. Combine soups and spread over top. Cover and refrigerate overnight. Allow to stand at room temperature for 1 hour before baking.
Bake for 40-45 minutes.
Sprinkle with crumbs and bake 15 minutes longer.
Serves 12-14.

Oven Baked Chicken Wings

Great family fare.

3	lb	chicken wings, cut in half, tips discarded	1.5 kg
2	Tbsp	soy sauce	30 mL
2	Tbsp	oil	30 mL
¼	cup	brown sugar	50 mL
1	Tbsp	chili powder	15 mL
1	Tbsp	celery seed	15 mL
1		can (10oz/284mL) tomato soup	1
⅓		soup can vinegar	⅓

Preheat broiler.

Baste chicken wings with a mixture of soy sauce and oil. Place on a broiler pan and sprinkle on the next 3 ingredients.

Broil for 5-7 minutes. Transfer wings to a baking dish and pour over combined soup and vinegar.

Reduce oven temperature to 325°F (160°C).

Bake for 1¼ hours.

Note: Chicken thighs may be substituted for wings.

Serves 4-6.

Chicken Chow Mein

3		chicken breasts, boned, skinned and cut into bite-size pieces	3
3		cloves garlic, minced	3
2	Tbsp	chopped fresh ginger	30 mL
2	Tbsp	vegetable oil	30 mL
4	cups	bean sprouts	1 L
2	cups	sliced mushrooms	500 mL
1		green pepper, chopped	1
1		red pepper, chopped	1
1		can (14oz/398mL) baby corn	1
1		can (8oz/227mL) sliced water chestnuts, drained	1
¼	cup	toasted almonds	50 mL
2	Tbsp	toasted sesame seeds	30 mL
1		pkg (14oz/397g) steam fried noodles	1

Stir-fry the first 3 ingredients in hot oil. Add the next 8 ingredients, continuing to stir-fry. Place noodles in a large colander. Pour a kettle of boiling water through. Mix noodles into first mixture then pour sauce over and mix again.

Sauce

½	cup	chicken stock	125 mL
2	Tbsp	sesame oil	30 mL
2	Tbsp	teriyaki sauce	30 mL
2	Tbsp	lemon juice	30 mL
1	Tbsp	black bean sauce	15 mL
1	tsp	chili sauce	5 mL

Combine all sauce ingredients, stirring well.
Serves 6.

Chinese Chicken

4	lb	chicken, cut up and skinned	2 kg
½	cup	soy sauce	125 mL
1	Tbsp	white wine or sherry	15 mL
1	Tbsp	grated fresh ginger	15 mL
1	tsp	dry mustard	5 mL
½	tsp	pepper	2 mL
2		cloves garlic, minced	2

Preheat oven to 350°F (180°C).
Place chicken in a container for marinating. Combine the remaining ingredients and pour over chicken. Marinate 2 hours or overnight in the refrigerator, turning several times.
Bake in a shallow casserole for 1 hour.
Serves 4.

Turkey Parmigiana

Flavour-packed turkey thighs.

4		turkey thigh cutlets	4
⅓	cup	flour	75 mL
1	Tbsp	vegetable oil	15 mL
1		can (14oz/398mL) Italian style tomato sauce salt and pepper garlic powder	1
1	cup	grated mozzarella cheese	250 mL
2	Tbsp	grated parmesan cheese	30 mL

Preheat oven to 350°F (180°c).
Dredge cutlets in flour. Sauté in oil until browned. Pour half the sauce into a baking dish, set cutlets on top, sprinkle with salt, pepper and garlic. Cover with remaining sauce and top with cheese. Bake for 35 minutes.
Serves 4.

Turkey Scallops

From skillet to table in just minutes.

4		turkey breast steaks	4
¼	cup	finely chopped onion	50 mL
6		mushrooms, sliced	6
2	Tbsp	oil, divided	30 mL
1	Tbsp	butter	15 mL
		flour for dredging turkey	
2	Tbsp	vermouth	30 mL
1		chicken bouillon cube	1
½	cup	water	125 mL
		freshly ground pepper	
		Veloutine	

Between a folded sheet of waxed paper, flatten each breast to ¼"
(.5cm). Dredge in flour. In frying pan, sauté onion and mushrooms
in 1 Tbsp (15mL) oil. Remove from pan. Add butter and 1 Tbsp
(15mL) oil to pan and sauté turkey steaks for about 5 minutes on
each side. Remove steaks and deglaze pan with vermouth, bouillon
cube and water. Bring to a boil, scraping up pan bits. Thicken
slightly with Veloutine. Return turkey and vegetables to pan and
sprinkle with pepper. Cover and simmer for about 8 minutes. Serve
with Stove Top Stuffing.
Serves 4.

Stuffed Turkey Roll

3	cups	chopped broccoli	750	mL
1½	lb	lean ground turkey	750	g
½		medium onion, finely minced	½	
1	cup	fine fresh breadcrumbs	250	mL
1	Tbsp	chopped parsley	15	mL
½	tsp	dried majoram	2	mL
½	tsp	ground pepper	2	mL
¼	tsp	sage	1	mL

Preheat oven to 350°F (180°C).

Blanch broccoli for 30 seconds in a pot of boiling water. Drain and plunge into ice water. Drain thoroughly, pat dry and set aside. Combine turkey and the remaining ingredients, mixing thoroughly. Place on a sheet of waxed paper and pat into an 8x15" (20x38cm) rectangle. Scatter broccoli over meat and roll up meat from the short end, jelly roll style, lifting with paper to ease rolling. Place seam side down in a greased baking pan.

Bake for 1 hour or until browned. Spoon tomato sauce over loaf. Pass remaining sauce.

Serves 8.

Tomato Sauce

1		onion, chopped	1
1		clove garlic, minced	1
1		can (19oz/540mL) tomatoes, crushed	1
2	Tbsp	chopped parsley	30 mL
½	tsp	oregano	2 mL

Combine all sauce ingredients in a saucepan. Bring to a boil, and simmer uncovered for 25 minutes, or until thickened.

Turkey Garbanzo Chili

A new interpretation of a classic.

¾	lb	ground turkey	375 g
2		medium onions, coarsely chopped	2
1	tsp	vegetable oil	5 mL
2		celery stalks, sliced	2
2		large carrots, sliced	2
1		green pepper, chopped	1
3		large cloves garlic, minced	3
2		cans (19oz/540mL) garbanzo beans, drained	2
1		can (28oz/750mL) stewed tomatoes	1
3	Tbsp	tomato paste	45 mL
3-4	Tbsp	chili powder, or to taste	45-60 mL
1	tsp	cumin	5 mL
1	tsp	oregano	5 mL
½	tsp	thyme	2 mL
1		bay leaf	1
¼	cup	chopped fresh parsley	50 mL

In a large heavy dutch oven, sauté the turkey and onion in oil for 3 minutes. Add celery and cook until meat is no longer pink. Add remaining ingredients, except parsley.
Cover and cook over low heat for 2 hours until flavours develop and chili is thick. Stir frequently. Remove bay leaf and sprinkle with parsley. Optional: Pass chopped avocado, green onions and grated cheddar.
Serves 6.

Stuffed Shells Siciliano

This tasty and attractive dish takes only minutes to prepare. A real family favourite.

1	lb	ground raw turkey or veal	500 g
1	cup	chopped onion	250 mL
1	cup	shredded zucchini	250 mL
2		cloves garlic, crushed	2
2	Tbsp	cracker crumbs	30 mL
		salt and pepper to taste	
1		can (19oz/540mL) tomatoes	1
1		can (14oz/398mL) tomato sauce	1
1	tsp	oregano	5 mL
1	tsp	basil	5 mL
½	tsp	tarragon	2 mL
¼	tsp	cayenne pepper	1 mL
¼	cup	parmesan cheese	50 mL
1	cup	shredded mozzarella cheese	250 mL
24		jumbo pasta seashells, cooked	24

Microwave the first 4 ingredients until cooked. Discard drained juices. Stir in cracker crumbs, salt and pepper. Set aside. Combine the next 6 ingredients and heat in microwave or on stovetop until bubbly. Stir a little less than half the tomato sauce into the meat along with the parmesan. Stuff shells. Spread a thin layer of the remaining sauce on the bottom of a 9x13" (22x34cm) baking dish, place stuffed shells in dish and spoon remaining sauce over. Sprinkle mozzarella over all.

Microwave 6-8 minutes and let stand 3 minutes or bake in 350°F (180°C) oven for 20 minutes.

Serves 6-8.

Zingy Cabbage Rolls

Tangy and delicious.

1		cabbage, cored	1

Filling

1½	lb	ground beef	750 g
2		onions, chopped	2
1	cup	uncooked minute rice	250 mL
1	cup	chili sauce	250 mL
1		clove garlic, crushed	1
1	tsp	savory	5 mL
		salt and pepper to taste	

Tomato Sauce

1		can (28oz/796mL) stewed tomatoes	1
1		can (10oz/284mL) tomato soup	1
½		can (10oz/284mL) water	½
¼	cup	vinegar	50 mL
¼	cup	brown sugar	50 mL
1	Tbsp	teriyaki sauce	15 mL
1	tsp	dry mustard	5 mL
½	tsp	cloves	2 mL
2		bay leaves	2

Preheat oven to 375°F(190°C).
Separate 12-16 cabbage leaves and boil for 5 minutes. Drain. Combine filling ingredients. Place ¼ cup (50mL) meat mixture on each leaf, roll up and skewer with toothpicks. Shred remainder of cabbage. Pour half tomato sauce in a 9x13"(22x34cm) baking dish. Add shredded cabbage and set rolls on top. Pour remaining sauce over and bake covered for 1 hour.
Note: The cored head of cabbage may be placed in a large pot of boiling water for 3-5 minutes for easier separation of leaves.
Serves 6-8.

Czech Goulash

This recipe comes from Otto Lowy, host of CBC's The Transcontinental radio program.

2		medium onions, chopped	2
2		cloves garlic, minced	2
¼	cup	vegetable oil	50 mL
2	lb	stewing beef, cut in 1" (2.5cm) cubes	1 kg
2	tsp	paprika	10 mL
1	tsp	allspice	5 mL
½	tsp	black pepper	2 mL
2		bay leaves	2
2	cups	water	500 mL
2	Tbsp	flour	30 mL
2		cubes beef bouillon	2
		chopped green pepper (optional)	

Sauté onion and garlic in oil until golden. Add beef cubes and spices. Simmer covered on low heat until meat is nearly tender. Add water, flour and bouillon. Continue cooking until meat is very tender. Add chopped green pepper if desired.
Serve with broad noodles.
Serves 4-6.

Sauced Rare Roast Beef

A delicious entrée from yesterday's roast.

½	lb	mushrooms, sliced	250 g
1	Tbsp	finely chopped onion	15 mL
3	Tbsp	butter	45 mL
½	cup	water	125 mL
¼	cup	red wine	50 mL
1	Tbsp	cornstarch	15 mL
1		bouillon cube	1
1	tsp	tomato paste	5 mL
1	tsp	kitchen bouquet seasoning	5 mL
¼	tsp	Worcestershire sauce	1 mL

thinly sliced rare roast beef
watercress for garnish (optional)

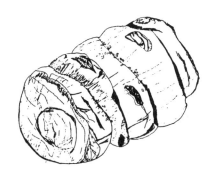

Sauté mushrooms and onion in butter, until golden, about 4 minutes.
Mix cornstarch with water and wine to blend. Add to mushrooms
along with remaining ingredients. Cook and stir until thickened.
Place sliced beef on a hot platter. Pour sauce over and garnish.
Note: Hot mashed potatoes piped around the platter edge add a
finishing touch.
Serves 4.

Encore Beef Enchiladas

Plan extra roast beef for this delicious dish.

1	Tbsp	vegetable oil	15 mL
1		large onion, sliced	1
1		large red pepper, cut in strips	1
1		green pepper, cut in strips	1
1		clove garlic, minced	1
2	cups	shredded roast beef	500 mL
1¾	cups	taco sauce, divided	425 mL
1	tsp	ground cumin	5 mL
¼	tsp	pepper	1 mL
8		(7"/18cm) flour tortillas	8
½	cup	sour cream	125 mL
1	cup	grated cheddar cheese	250 mL
3	Tbsp	chopped green onions	45 mL

Preheat oven to 350°F (180°C).

Heat oil over medium heat, add onion and cook 2 minutes, add peppers and garlic and cook and stir for 3 minutes. Remove from heat and stir in beef, ¾ cup (175mL) taco sauce, cumin and pepper. Place mixture down centre of each tortilla. Overlap edges and place in a greased baking dish, overlapped edges up. Spoon remaining sauce over. Spoon sour cream down centre of tortillas and sprinkle with cheese.

Bake for 30 minutes, until hot. Sprinkle onions over cheese and serve.

Serves 8.

Mock Taco Casserole

A delicious and easy casserole for "kids" of all ages.

1	lb	ground beef	500	g
1		can (28oz/796mL) stewed tomatoes, chopped	1	
2		cloves garlic, minced	2	
1	Tbsp	chili powder	15	mL
½	tsp	cumin	2	mL
½	tsp	oregano	2	mL
¼	tsp	ground pepper	1	mL
1		pkg (12oz/375g) plain taco chips	1	
2		cans (10oz/284mL) enchilada bean dip	2	
1		can (4oz/114mL) chopped green chilies, drained	1	
1		jar (8oz/227mL) mild taco sauce	1	
1	cup	chopped onion	250	mL
1	cup	grated cheddar cheese	250	mL
1	cup	grated Monterey Jack cheese	250	mL

Preheat oven to 325°F (160°C).

Brown meat in a large frying pan. Add the next 6 ingredients and simmer, uncovered 15 minutes. Line bottom of a 9x13" (22x34cm) baking dish with broken taco chips. Spread with bean dip then layer remaining ingredients in order given. Top with tomato meat mixture. Bake for 30 minutes.

Serve with shredded lettuce, chopped tomatoes and more taco sauce if desired.

Serves 8.

Sweet and Sour Pork

This easy skillet dish is sure to please every family member.
Prepare the sauce ahead.

1½	lb	lean pork, cubed	750 g
1	Tbsp	oil	15 mL
2		stalks celery, chopped	2
1		medium onion, sliced	1
1		green pepper, in chunks	1
1	cup	pineapple chunks	250 mL
2	cups	sweet and sour sauce	500 mL

In a skillet, brown pork cubes in oil. Add vegetables and sauté for 5 minutes. Add pineapple and sweet and sour sauce, simmer for 15 minutes. Serve over rice.
Serves 6.

Sweet and Sour Sauce

2	cups	apple juice	500 mL
2	cups	beef broth	500 mL
⅔	cup	sugar	150 mL
½	cup	cider vinegar	125 mL
¼	cup	soy sauce	50 mL
2	Tbsp	minced fresh ginger	30 mL
½	cup	cornstarch	125 mL
⅔	cup	water	150 mL

In a medium saucepan, bring the first 6 ingredients to a boil. Mix cornstarch with water and add to boiling mixture, stirring constantly until thickened, about 1 minute. Sauce can be refrigerated up to 2 weeks or frozen for 2 months.
Yields 5-6 cups.

Citrus Chops

4		loin pork chops, trimmed of fat	4
2	Tbsp	soy sauce	30 mL
		pepper and garlic powder to taste	
4		thin lemon slices	4
4		thin orange slices	4
4		thin onion slices	4
½	cup	orange juice	125 mL
2	tsp	cornstarch	10 mL
2	tsp	honey	10 mL

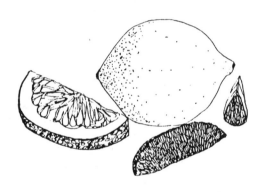

Preheat oven to 350°F (180°C).

Brush both sides of chops with soy sauce. Sprinkle with pepper and garlic. Arrange in a single layer in a baking pan and top each chop with orange, lemon and onion slices. Combine the remaining ingredients and pour over.

Bake for 1 hour, basting occasionally with sauce. Cover if chops seem to be drying.

Serves 4.

Hot Pasta with Cold Sauce

This delightful recipe comes from Executive Chef Elio Guarnori of the Hotel Vancouver.

3		medium tomatoes, peeled, seeded and finely chopped	3
1		green pepper, finely chopped	1
1		bunch green onions, chopped	1
12		pitted ripe olives, chopped	12
1		clove garlic, minced (optional)	1
2	Tbsp	chopped fresh parsley	30 mL
1	Tbsp	chopped fresh basil	15 mL
½	cup	chopped pecans	125 mL
4	Tbsp	virgin olive oil	60 mL
		freshly ground black pepper	
12	oz	cooked pasta of your choice	375 g

Mix all the sauce ingredients and let stand for 2 hours or longer. Spoon over the hot pasta and serve.
Serves 4.

Tortellini in Mushroom Sauce

1	lb	mushrooms, sliced	500 g
3		cloves garlic, minced	3
1	Tbsp	butter	15 mL
¼	cup	fresh basil, chopped	50 mL
6	oz	cream cheese, softened	170 g
¾	cup	milk	175 mL
		ground pepper	
12	oz	fresh or frozen tortellini, cooked	375 g

Sauté mushrooms and garlic in butter until browned. Add the next 4 ingredients and stir to combine. Pour over cooked tortellini.
Serves 4.

Garden Fresh Fettuccine

Juicy ripe tomatoes and fresh herbs are the base for this saucy creation.

12	oz	fresh spinach fettuccine, cooked according to package directions	375 g
2	Tbsp	vegetable oil	30 mL
1		onion, chopped	1
6		tomatoes, coarsely chopped	6
1		large red pepper, cut in strips	1
2		cloves garlic, minced	2
¾	cup	chopped fresh basil	175 mL
¼	cup	chopped parsley	50 mL
½	tsp	sugar	2 mL
½	tsp	pepper salt to taste	2 mL
⅓	cup	grated parmesan cheese	75 mL

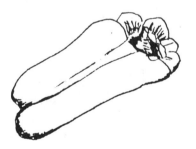

Heat oil, add onion and cook for 5 minutes. Add tomatoes, pepper strips and garlic and cook for 1 to 2 minutes. Add the next 5 ingredients, cook and stir until hot and bubbly. Spoon over hot fettuccine. Sprinkle with cheese.
Serves 4.

Tamale Pie

This make ahead open-faced pie fills the bill.

Filling

1		medium onion, chopped	1
1		can (7oz/213mL) diced green chilies	1
1	Tbsp	vegetable oil	15 mL
1½	lb	lean ground beef	750 g
1	Tbsp	chili powder	15 mL
1	cup	red taco sauce	250 mL
3	cups	grated cheddar cheese	750 mL
		cornmeal crust	
1		ripe avocado, peeled and sliced	1

Crust

1½	cups	cornmeal	375 mL
3½	cups	water	875 mL
½	tsp	ground cumin	2 mL
¼	tsp	cayenne	1 mL

Preheat oven to 350°F (180°C).
Combine crust ingredients in a saucepan and bring to a boil. Cook and stir for 8-10 minutes until mixture thickens enough to leave a path when a spoon is drawn through it. Spread mixture over bottom and 1" (2.5cm) up sides of a shallow, ungreased 3 qt (3L) casserole. For filling, sauté onion and chilies in oil until onion is soft and tender. Remove from pan and set aside. Brown meat with chili powder until meat is no longer pink. Skim off any fat. Stir in onion mixture, half the taco sauce and half the cheese. Spoon into crust. If made ahead, cover and chill overnight.
Bake uncovered for 30-40 minutes until hot in the centre. Top with remaining cheese and bake until melted, about 5 minutes. Garnish with avocado. Serve with remaining sauce.
Serves 6.

Breads

Cranberry Plus Muffins

2	cups	flour	500 mL
¾	cup	sugar	175 mL
2	tsp	baking soda	10 mL
2	tsp	cinnamon	10 mL
½	tsp	salt	2 mL
1¼	cups	grated carrots	300 mL
½	cup	raisins	125 mL
½	cup	chopped nuts	125 mL
½	cup	flaked coconut	125 mL
1		medium apple, peeled and grated	1
3		eggs	3
¾	cup	vegetable oil	175 mL
2	tsp	vanilla	10 mL
1¼	cups	fresh (or frozen) cranberries	300 mL

Preheat oven to 350°F (180°C).
Combine the first 10 ingredients in a large mixing bowl. Beat eggs, oil and vanilla in a small bowl. Add to dry ingredients, stirring just to moisten. Stir in cranberries. Fill large greased muffin cups ¾ full. Bake for 20-25 minutes.
Makes 18 muffins.

Pumpkin Muffins

Moist and delicious.

¾	cup	natural bran	175 mL
¾	cup	whole wheat flour	175 mL
½	cup	sugar	125 mL
1½	tsp	cinnamon	7 mL
1	tsp	baking powder	5 mL
1	tsp	baking soda	5 mL
½	tsp	salt	2 mL
1	cup	raisins	250 mL
1	cup	canned pumpkin or mashed fresh	250 mL
2		eggs	2
½	cup	vegetable oil	125 mL
½	cup	plain yogurt or buttermilk	125 mL

Preheat oven to 400°F (200°C).
In a bowl combine the first 8 ingredients, toss to mix. Combine the remaining ingredients and add to the first mixture. Stir just to blend. Spoon into paper-lined muffin tins.
Bake for 25 minutes or until firm to the touch.
Makes 12 muffins.

Raisin Muffins

1¼	cups	raisins	300	mL
2	cups	water	500	mL
¼	cup	butter	50	mL
⅓	cup	brown sugar	75	mL
1		egg	1	
½	tsp	vanilla	2	mL
1½	cups	flour	375	mL
1	tsp	soda	5	mL

Preheat oven to 375°F (190°C).
Boil raisins and water for 20 minutes. Drain and cool, reserving
¾ cup (175mL) liquid. Cream butter and sugar. Add egg and vanilla,
beating well. Stir in dry ingredients, raisins and reserved raisin
water. Spoon into paper-lined muffin cups.
Bake for 18 minutes.
Makes 10 muffins.

Carrot Cheesecake Muffins

A yummy muffin with a surprise cheese centre.

1		pkg (4oz/125g) cream cheese, softened	1	
2	Tbsp	sugar	30	mL
½	tsp	finely grated orange rind	2	mL
⅓	cup	butter, softened	75	mL
½	cup	brown sugar	125	mL
2		eggs	2	
2	Tbsp	frozen orange juice concentrate	30	mL
½	cup	canned evaporated milk	125	mL
1	tsp	finely grated orange rind	5	mL
1¼	cups	grated carrot	300	mL
½	cup	raisins	125	mL
½	cup	chopped walnuts	125	mL
1¼	cups	flour	300	mL
1	tsp	baking powder	5	mL
½	tsp	cinnamon	2	mL

Preheat oven to 350°F (180°C).
For filling, cream the first 3 ingredients in a small bowl until smooth. Set aside.
Cream together butter and sugar until light. Beat in the next 3 ingredients. Stir in orange rind, carrot, raisins and walnuts, mixing well. In a large bowl combine dry ingredients. Add carrot mixture, stirring until just moistened. Spoon 2 Tbsp (30mL) batter into each oiled or paper-lined muffin cup. Spoon 1 Tbsp (15mL) cream cheese mixture on top. Cover with remaining batter.
Bake for 20 minutes or until top is springy.
Makes 12 muffins.

Fruit and Nut Muffins

These wholesome nutritious muffins are made without sugar.
Use your imagination and vary the fruit.

1		apple, cored and chopped	1
½	cup	pitted prunes	125 mL
½	cup	pitted dates	125 mL
¼	cup	boiling water	50 mL
3		eggs, beaten	3
2		bananas, mashed	2
¼	cup	soft butter	50 mL
¼	cup	orange juice	50 mL
1	tsp	vanilla	5 mL
1½	cups	wholewheat flour	375 mL
1	cup	rolled oats	250 mL
½	cup	skim milk powder	125 mL
2	tsp	baking powder	10 mL
1	tsp	baking soda	5 mL
¼	tsp	salt	1 mL
½	cup	unsweetened coconut	125 mL
½	cup	chopped walnuts or sunflower seeds	125 mL

Preheat oven to 350°F (180°C).
Combine the first 4 ingredients in a food processor and process very
briefly. Place in a bowl and add the next 5 ingredients, mixing well.
In a large bowl combine the remaining ingredients. Make a well in
centre and add fruit mixture, stirring to blend. Spoon into greased
muffin tins.
Bake for 20-25 minutes.
Makes 12 giant muffins.

Irresistible Orange Scones

Wonderful for breakfast or serve with soup or a salad for lunch.

2¼	cups	flour	550 mL
½	cup	quick oats	125 mL
½	cup	oat bran	125 mL
4	tsp	baking powder	20 mL
½	tsp	baking soda	2 mL
⅓	cup	butter	75 mL
¼	cup	brown sugar	50 mL
½	cup	currants or raisins	125 mL
1½	Tbsp	grated orange peel	22 mL
½	cup	orange juice	125 mL
¼	cup	buttermilk	50 mL
1		egg	1

Preheat oven to 400°F (200°C).
Stir together the first 5 ingredients. With a pastry blender cut in the butter until the mixture resembles fine crumbs. Add the next 3 ingredients and stir to combine. Mix together the remaining ingredients and pour over flour mixture. Stir with a fork until moistened. Turn dough out onto a lightly floured board and knead five or six times (it will be sticky). Divide in half. Form each half into a 6" (15cm) circle on a lightly greased cookie sheet. Deeply score each circle into 6 wedges.
Bake for 20-25 minutes.
Makes 12 scones.

New England Gingerbread

Surprise! Wonderful gingerbread without ginger!

¾	cup	dark molasses	175 mL
½	cup	butter	125 mL
½	cup	boiling water	125 mL
1		egg	1
1½	cups	flour	375 mL
1	tsp	baking soda	5 mL
¾	tsp	cinnamon	3 mL
½	tsp	cloves	2 mL
½	tsp	nutmeg	2 mL

Preheat oven to 350°F (180°C).
Combine the first 3 ingredients in a saucepan. Stir over low heat until melted. Remove from heat and add the remaining ingredients, mixing well. Pour into a lightly oiled 9" (22cm) square pan.
Bake for 30 minutes.
Note: Recipe may be doubled. Use a 9x13" (22x34cm) pan and bake for 40 minutes.
Serves 6-8.

Apple Cake

Delicious served warm.

1	cup	sugar	250 mL
¼	cup	butter	50 mL
1		egg	1
1	cup	flour	250 mL
1	tsp	baking soda	5 mL
1	tsp	cinnamon	5 mL
½	tsp	nutmeg	2 mL
2½	cups	diced apple	625 mL
½	cup	chopped walnuts	125 mL
2	Tbsp	hot water	30 mL
1	tsp	vanilla	5 mL

Preheat oven to 350°F (180°C).
Cream butter and sugar, add egg and beat. Stir in dry ingredients then mix in remaining ingredients. Pour into a greased 8"(19cm) square pan.
Bake for 40-45 minutes.
Note: May be baked in a pie plate and cut in wedges.
Serves 8.

Apricot and Prune Coffeecake

¾	cup	dried apricots, packed	175 mL
¾	cup	dried prunes, packed	175 mL
1½	cups	boiling water	375 mL
⅔	cup	brown sugar	150 mL
1	Tbsp	flour	15 mL
1	Tbsp	cinnamon	15 mL
¾	cup	shortening, softened	175 mL
¾	cup	white sugar	175 mL
2		eggs	2
2	cups	flour	500 mL
2	tsp	baking powder	10 mL
½	tsp	salt	2 mL
¾	cup	milk	175 mL
1	tsp	vanilla	5 mL
⅓	cup	butter or margarine, melted	75 mL
⅓	cup	chopped walnuts or pecans	75 mL

Preheat oven to 350°F (180°C).
Pour boiling water over fruit and let stand 10 minutes. Drain, chop and set fruit aside. Combine the next 3 ingredients and set aside. In a large bowl cream shortening and sugar until light and fluffy. Beat in eggs, one at a time, beating well after each. Combine the next 3 ingredients and mix into creamed mixture alternately (in 3 additions) with the milk and vanilla. Fold in the reserved fruit. Pour ⅓ of batter into a greased and floured 9" (22cm) tube pan. Sprinkle with half the brown sugar mixture and drizzle half the butter over. Repeat. Pour on remaining batter and sprinkle with nuts.
Bake for 55 minutes or until cake tester comes out clean. Cool for 30 minutes before removing from pan.
Serves 10-12.

Sherried Zucchini Bread

Sherry gives a nice flavour to this moist loaf.

3		eggs	3
1	cup	brown sugar	250 mL
¾	cup	oil	175 mL
1	tsp	vanilla	5 mL
2	cups	grated zucchini	500 mL
3	cups	flour	750 mL
1	tsp	baking powder	5 mL
1	tsp	baking soda	5 mL
½	tsp	salt	2 mL
½	tsp	cinnamon, optional	2 mL
1½	cups	raisins	375 mL
⅓	cup	sherry	75 mL
½	cup	chopped walnuts	125 mL

Preheat oven to 325°F (160°C).
Soak raisins in the sherry while preparing the rest of the recipe.
Beat together the first 4 ingredients. Stir in zucchini and sifted dry
ingredients. Add raisins, sherry and nuts, stirring only to blend.
Spoon into 2 greased and floured loaf pans.
Bake for 1 hour.
Makes 2 loaves.

One Bowl Date Loaf

A flavour-packed moist loaf.

½	lb	dates, chopped	250 g
1	tsp	baking soda	5 mL
1	cup	boiling water	250 mL
2	Tbsp	butter	30 mL
1		egg	1
1	tsp	vanilla	5 mL
1	cup	brown sugar	250 mL
⅔	cup	chopped walnuts	150 mL
1½	cups	flour	375 mL

Preheat oven to 325°F (160°C).

Place dates in a bowl, sprinkle with soda and pour boiling water over. Stir in butter to melt. Beat in egg, vanilla and brown sugar. Stir in nuts then flour until combined. Pour into a greased and floured 5x9" (13x23cm) loaf pan.

Bake for 1 hour until cake tester, inserted near centre, comes out clean.

Makes 1 loaf.

Orange Loaf

A wonderful moist fruity loaf. Double the recipe and tuck one in the freezer.

1	cup	orange juice	250 mL
		thin rind of 1 extra large	
		or 2 medium oranges	
1	cup	raisins	250 mL
1	cup	sugar	250 mL
2	Tbsp	margarine, melted	30 mL
1	tsp	vanilla	5 mL
1		egg, lightly beaten	1
2	cups	flour	500 mL
1	tsp	baking powder	5 mL
½	tsp	soda	2 mL
½	cup	chopped walnuts	125 mL

Preheat oven to 350°F (180°C).
Pour juice into a blender, add orange rind and process until rind is in small chunks. Add raisins and chop slightly. Pour mixture into a bowl and stir in the next 4 ingredients. Mix in the dry ingredients blending thoroughly. Stir in nuts. Pour into a greased and floured 5x9" (13x23cm) loaf pan.
Bake for 1 hour or until cake tester inserted near centre comes out clean.
Makes 1 loaf.

Pumpkin Loaf

An easy to make harvest loaf.

2⅓	cups	tea biscuit mix	575 mL
1¼	cups	sugar	300 mL
1	cup	canned pumpkin	250 mL
⅓	cup	oil	75 mL
3		eggs	3
2	tsp	cinnamon	10 mL
½	cup	raisins	125 mL
½	cup	chopped pecans (optional)	125 mL

Preheat oven to 350°F (180°C).
Thoroughly mix together the first 6 ingredients. Stir in the raisins and nuts. Spoon into a greased 5x9" (13x23cm) loaf pan.
Bake for 50-55 minutes or until a cake tester, inserted near centre, comes out clean. Cool.
Makes 1 loaf.

Tea Biscuit Mix

Keep this mix in a tightly closed container in the refrigerator.

6	cups	flour	1.5 L
¼	cup	baking powder	50 mL
1	Tbsp	sugar	15 mL
1	tsp	cream of tartar	5 mL
1	tsp	salt	5 mL
1	cup	cold shortening or margarine	250 mL

Sift dry ingredients together. Cut in shortening until mixture resembles fine bread crumbs.
Note: For 12 tea biscuits, stir ⅔ cup (150mL) of milk into 2 cups (500mL) of mix. Turn dough out onto lightly floured board, and knead 7-8 times. Pat or roll dough to ¾" (2cm) thick and cut with a 2" (5cm) round floured cutter.
Bake at 425°F (220°C) for 12 minutes or until lightly browned.

Pull Apart Herb Loaf

1		pkg refrigerated crescent rolls	1
2	Tbsp	butter, softened	30 mL
¼	tsp	basil	1 mL
¼	tsp	oregano	1 mL
⅛	tsp	garlic powder	.5 mL

Preheat oven to 350°F (180°C).
Remove crescent dough from can. Do not unroll. Place roll seam side down on an ungreased baking sheet. With a serrated knife, partially cut roll into 12 slices to within ⅛" (.3cm) of bottom. Gently pull slices alternately to left and to right to form the loaf.
Bake for 20-25 minutes or until golden brown.
Combine the remaining ingredients and brush over hot loaf. Serve immediately.
Serves 4.

Buttermilk Bread

A quick mix bread that goes well with soup or a salad.

2½	cups	white flour	625 mL
5	cups	whole wheat flour	1.25 L
½	cup	sugar	125 mL
1½	Tbsp	soda	22 mL
1	Tbsp	salt	15 mL
1	qt	buttermilk	1 L

Preheat oven to 350°F (180°C).
Mix the first 5 ingredients together. Add buttermilk, a little at a time, mixing thoroughly. Let batter stand for 30 minutes. Divide batter among 3 greased and floured 5x9" (13x23cm) loaf pans.
Bake for 50-60 minutes.
Makes 3 loaves.

No Wait Wheat Oat Bread

1½	cups	oatmeal	375 mL
3		pkg rapidmix yeast	3
4	cups	warm water	1 L
2	Tbsp	honey	30 mL
¼	cup	honey	50 mL
¼	cup	oil	50 mL
1	Tbsp	salt	15 mL
¼	cup	wheat germ	50 mL
1	cup	soy grits	250 mL
½	cup	sunflower seeds (optional)	125 mL
7	cups	whole wheat flour	1.75 L

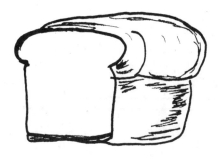

Preheat oven to 275°F (140°C).

Warm oatmeal in oven. In a large bowl dissolve yeast and honey in warm water. Let stand 10 minutes until foamy. Add the next 3 ingredients and warmed oatmeal. Let stand a few minutes. Mix in the remaining ingredients, kneading in last cup of flour until dough is elastic. Divide dough in half and form into 2 loaves. Place in 2 large oiled loaf pans.

Bake for 15 minutes. Increase oven temperature to 350°F (180°C) and bake for 40 minutes.

Makes 2 loaves.

Yorkshire Pudding

High and puffy yet low in cholesterol.

2		egg whites	2
1	cup	skim milk	250 mL
½	cup	defrosted "egg beaters" or other egg substitute	125 mL
1	Tbsp	safflower oil	15 mL
½	tsp	salt substitute	2 mL
1	cup	flour	250 mL
3	Tbsp	safflower oil for muffin cups	45 mL

Preheat oven to 500°F (260°C).

Place the first 5 ingredients in a blender. Process, adding flour slowly. For the next 10 minutes, while preparing pans, turn blender on for a few seconds. Pour 1 tsp (5mL) oil into each of 9 muffin cups, spreading oil around sides and top of pan. Place pan in oven until oil is bubbling hot. Whirl blender one last time then fill muffin cups ¾ full.

Bake for 15 minutes then reduce heat to 350°F (180°C) and bake 15 minutes longer.

Makes 9 individual Yorkshires.

Crescent Rolls

1		pkg traditional yeast	1	
½	cup	warm milk	125	mL
1	tsp	sugar	5	mL
4	cups	flour	1	L
¼	cup	sugar	50	mL
1	tsp	salt	5	mL
½	cup	vegetable shortening	125	mL
2		eggs, beaten	2	
½	cup	warm milk	125	mL

Preheat oven to 375°F (190°C).
Dissolve yeast in the warm milk and sugar, set aside. Sift together the next 3 ingredients. Mix in the shortening with fingertips or pastry cutter. Stir in the remaining ingredients and the foamy yeast mixture. Let rise until double in bulk, about 1 hour. Divide dough in half and roll out in 2 circles the size of a dinner plate. Cut each circle into 12 pie shapes and brush with melted butter. Roll up each wedge from wide end. Place rolls on baking sheet and let rise for 1 hour. Bake for 20 minutes or until light brown.
Makes 24 rolls.

Banana Split Dessert

A spectacular dessert!

1¼	cups	graham wafer crumbs	300	mL
⅓	cup	butter, melted	75	mL
2	cups	icing sugar	500	mL
¾	cup	butter	175	mL
2		eggs	2	
4-7		bananas, sliced lengthwise	4-7	
1		can (19oz/540mL) crushed pineapple, drained	1	
1		pkg (20oz/600g) frozen unsweetened strawberries, thawed and drained, or 4 cups (1L) fresh berries	1	
1	cup	whipping cream, whipped	250	mL
1		envelope Dream Whip, whipped according to directions	1	

Combine graham wafer crumbs and butter. Press into a 9x13" (22x34cm) pan. Beat the next 3 ingredients together for about 5 minutes or until light and fluffy. Spread over the base. Layer bananas next, followed by pineapple, then strawberries. Combine whipped cream with Dream Whip and spread on top. Refrigerate. Serves 10-12.

Sherried Fruit

Excellent! A light easy way to end a meal.

¾	cup	honey	175 mL
2	Tbsp	lemon juice	30 mL
2	Tbsp	orange juice	30 mL
1	Tbsp	grated lemon rind	15 mL
½	cup	sherry	125 mL
1		pkg (10oz/300g) frozen strawberries	1
1	cup	sliced pears, fresh or canned	250 mL
1	cup	sliced peaches, fresh or canned	250 mL
1	cup	cubed pineapple, fresh or canned	250 mL
1	cup	green seedless grapes, halved to absorb colour other fruits in season *eg* papaya, mango, kiwi - added before serving	250 mL

Combine the first 4 ingredients in a saucepan over medium heat. Cook and stir for 5 minutes. Add sherry and pour over frozen strawberries. Add the remaining fruit. Allow to stand for at least 4 hours stirring occasionally.
Serves 8.

Berries with Pineapple Cream

A light fresh tasting dessert.

1½	cups	chilled pineapple juice	375 mL
1½	cups	plain yogurt	375 mL
1		pkg (3oz/92g) vanilla instant pudding	1
4	cups	sliced strawberries	1 L
8		whole strawberries	8

Combine pineapple juice and yogurt in a small deep bowl. Add pudding mix and beat on low speed with an electric mixer until smooth, about 2 minutes. Divide sliced berries among dessert glasses and spoon pineapple mixture over the top. Garnish each dessert with a whole berry.
Serves 8.

Microwave Baked Apples

4		tart apples, cored	4
⅓	cup	mincemeat	75 mL
¼	cup	apple juice	50 mL
2	Tbsp	brown sugar	30 mL
1	tsp	cinnamon	5 mL
		pinch of cloves	

Peel ⅓ of the skin from around the top of each apple.
Stuff apples with mincemeat and place in a shallow microwave dish.
Combine remaining ingredients and pour over apples.
Microwave on medium high for 5 minutes or until cooked. Let rest for 5 minutes. Baste with sauce in dish. Serve with ice cream if desired.
Serves 4.

Apple Amaretto Crisp

A new twist to an old standby.

6		medium apples, peeled, cored and cut into ½" (1.3cm) wedges	6
¼	cup	Amaretto or almond liqueur	50 mL
¾	cup	brown sugar	175 mL
¾	cup	oatmeal	175 mL
½	cup	flour	125 mL
¼	cup	coarsely chopped almonds	50 mL
¼	tsp	cinnamon	1 mL
½	cup	cold butter	125 mL

Preheat oven to 350°F(180°C).
Place apple slices in an oiled casserole. Stir in liqueur. Combine the next 5 ingredients in a bowl. Cut in butter with pastry blender until mixture is crumbly. Spread over apples and pat gently.
Bake uncovered for 45 minutes.
Serves 6.

Special Fruit Bowl

Wonderful for a large gathering.

2		cans (14oz/398mL) crushed pineapple, drained	2
2	cups	seedless green grapes	500 mL
2	cups	sliced fresh strawberries	500 mL
1		pkg (3½oz/100g) pecan halves	1
5	cups	miniature marshmallows	1.25 L

Sauce

4		egg yolks	4
½	cup	sweetened condensed milk	125 mL
½	tsp	prepared mustard	2 mL
		juice of 1 lemon	
2	cups	whipping cream, whipped	500 mL

Place the first 5 ingredients in a large glass bowl. To prepare sauce, combine the first 3 ingredients in a double boiler, cooking and stirring until thick. Remove from heat and add lemon juice. Cool. Fold whipped cream into sauce mixture. Gently combine sauce and fruit. Garnish with fresh fruit. Cover with plastic wrap and refrigerate for 24 hours.
Serves 20 or more.

Almond Toffee Apple Cake

A crown of apples and chewy toffee almonds make this cake irresistible.

¾	cup	butter	175 mL
1	cup	sugar	250 mL
2		large eggs	2
2	cups	flour	500 mL
2	tsp	baking powder	10 mL
1-2		Granny Smith apples, quartered, cored, peeled, thinly sliced	1-2

Preheat oven to 350°F (180°C).
In a large bowl, cream butter and sugar. Add eggs, one at a time, beating well after each. Add flour and baking powder, mixing until blended. Spread batter in a lightly oiled 9" (22cm) spring form pan. Arrange apple slices on batter in circular fashion, overlapping slightly, leaving centre uncovered.
Bake for 50-60 minutes until centre of cake is lightly brown and springy to touch.

Almond Toffee Topping

6	Tbsp	butter	90 mL
½	cup	sugar	125 mL
1	Tbsp	flour	15 mL
1	cup	sliced almonds	250 mL

While cake is baking, prepare topping. Melt butter in a saucepan over medium heat. Add sugar and flour, stirring until blended and bubbly. Stir in almonds. Spread hot topping over hot cake and return to oven until topping is golden, about 15 minutes. Be careful not to overcook. Serve warm or cool.
Makes 12 wedges.

Windsong Cake

It's a breeze to make.

1½	cups	sifted cake flour	375 mL
1	tsp	baking powder	5 mL
½	tsp	salt	2 mL
3		egg yolks	3
¾	cup	cold water	175 mL
1¼	cups	sugar	300 mL
3		egg whites	3
1½	tsp	vanilla, almond or lemon flavouring	7 mL

Preheat oven to 325°F (160°C).

Sift together twice, the first 3 ingredients. In a large bowl beat egg yolks until frothy. Add water and continue beating at high speed until bowl is nearly full of liquid and bubbles are very small, about 5 minutes. Add sugar gradually, beating well after each addition. Add dry ingredients slowly, beating constantly. Beat egg whites until stiff but not dry. Fold into batter quickly along with flavouring. Pour into an ungreased 10" (25cm) tube pan.

Bake for about 50 minutes. Invert pan immediately and let cool in pan. When ready to serve dust with icing sugar.

Serves 8-10.

UBC Ponderosa Cake

This cake was made famous by the UBC Ponderosa Cafeteria.

1	cup	butter	250 mL
2	cups	sugar	500 mL
2		eggs	2
1	tsp	vanilla	5 mL
3	cups	mashed bananas (about 6-7)	750 mL
3	cups	flour	750 mL
2	tsp	baking powder	10 mL
2	tsp	baking soda	10 mL
1	cup	light sour cream	250 mL

Topping

½	cup	brown sugar	125 mL
1	tsp	cinnamon	5 mL
1½	cups	chocolate chips	375 mL

Preheat oven to 350°F (180°C).
Cream butter and sugar. Beat in the next 3 ingredients. Add dry ingredients alternately with sour cream. Spread half the batter in a lightly oiled 9x13" (22x34cm) cake pan. Sprinkle on half the topping and half the chocolate chips. Repeat.
Bake for 50-65 minutes.
Makes a large cake.

Lite Chocolate Zucchini Cake

Easy to make and great to eat.

½	cup	light margarine	125 mL
½	cup	light oil	125 mL
1¾	cups	sugar	425 mL
2		eggs	2
½	cup	skim milk	125 mL
2	Tbsp	vinegar	30 mL
1	tsp	vanilla	5 mL
2½	cups	flour	625 mL
¼	cup	carob powder	50 mL
1	tsp	soda	5 mL
1	tsp	baking powder	5 mL
½	tsp	salt	2 mL
½	tsp	cinnamon	2 mL
⅛	tsp	cloves	.5 mL
2	cups	finely chopped unpeeled zucchini	500 mL
¾	cup	pecans	175 mL
½	cup	carob chips	125 mL

Preheat oven to 325°F (160°C).
In a large mixing bowl beat together the first 14 ingredients. Add the remaining ingredients mixing thoroughly. Pour into a paper-lined 9x13" (22x34cm) pan.
Bake for 50 minutes or until top is springy.
Serves 12.

Hallowe'en Cake

This pumpkin chiffon cake is a hit any time of the year.

7		egg yolks	7
¾	cup	canned pumpkin	175 mL
½	cup	oil	125 mL
½	cup	cold water	125 mL
2	cups	flour	500 mL
1½	cups	sugar	375 mL
1	Tbsp	baking powder	15 mL
1	tsp	cinnamon	5 mL
1	tsp	salt (optional)	5 mL
½	tsp	cloves	2 mL
½	tsp	nutmeg	2 mL
7		egg whites	7
½	tsp	cream of tartar	2 mL

Preheat oven to 350°F (180°C).
Beat together the first 4 ingredients in a large mixing bowl. Combine the next 7 ingredients and add to pumpkin mixture, blending well. Beat egg whites and cream of tartar until very stiff. Fold into batter. Pour into an ungreased tube pan.
Bake for 60-70 minutes until top is cracked and very dry. Turn cake upside down and cool in pan.
Serves 10-12.

Icing suggestions:
1. Round the sides off cooled cake and place the trimmings into the centre to fill the hole. Ice with orange icing and decorate like a large pumpkin, using black licorice for stem, etc.
2. Ice with butter icing and cover with finely chopped walnuts.

Iced Pear and Apricot Soufflé

Serve with Raspberry Sauce, page 159.

2		cans (28oz/796mL) pear halves, no sugar added, well drained	2
2		envelopes unflavoured gelatin	2
½	cup	sugar	125 mL
4		egg yolks	4
10		dried apricots, finely minced	10
		grated peel of 2 lemons	
3	Tbsp	brandy	45 mL
2	Tbsp	lemon juice	30 mL
6		egg whites	6
⅛	tsp	salt	.5 mL
¼	cup	sugar	50 mL

Cut 4 pear halves into ¼" (5mm) dice. Set aside. Purée remaining pears in blender. Add gelatin. Transfer purée to a large saucepan, cooking and occasionally stirring for 30 minutes or until reduced to about 2 cups. Do not brown. Beat sugar and egg yolks until thick. Add apricots and lemon peel, beating until pale in colour. Add 2 Tbsp (30mL) hot purée, blending well. Add remaining purée, brandy and lemon juice. Mix well. Fold in diced pear. Refrigerate, stirring occasionally, until mixture has cooled and begins to thicken. Beat egg whites until foamy. Add salt and continue beating until whites are stiff and glossy. Add sugar and beat for 5 seconds more. Fold into pear mixture gently but thoroughly. Spoon into large soufflé dish. Refrigerate overnight or until completely set. Garnish with seasonal fruit.
Serves 12.

Almond Mocha Mousse

Divine!

2		egg whites	2	
1	Tbsp	instant coffee	15	mL
2	Tbsp	sugar	30	mL
1	cup	whipping cream	250	mL
¼	cup	sugar	50	mL
1	Tbsp	coffee liqueur (optional)	15	mL
1	tsp	vanilla	5	mL
¼	cup	chopped toasted almonds	50	mL

Beat egg whites and coffee until stiff. Beat in sugar gradually. In a separate bowl beat cream until it holds firm peaks. Slowly beat in remaining ingredients. Fold cream into egg white mixture. Spoon into parfait or dessert dishes and freeze 2 hours.
Serves 8.

Strawberry Mousse

Wonderful in meringue shells.

1		envelope unflavoured gelatin	1	
1		package (15oz/450g) frozen strawberries	1	
2		egg whites	2	
1½	cups	skim milk	375	mL
1	tsp	lemon juice	5	mL
1	Tbsp	slivered almonds, toasted (optional)	15	mL

Partially thaw berries.
Pour ½ cup (125mL) of cold milk into the blender. Sprinkle gelatin over and let stand 3 minutes. Scald remaining milk and add to the blender. Process 1 minute. Add egg whites, blend. Add lemon juice and strawberries. Process 1 minute. Pour into individual serving dishes and refrigerate until set, 2-3 hours. Garnish with almonds.
Serves 4-6.

Cherry Parfait

Don't be put off by the ingredients. This is a winner!

1	can (19oz/540mL) cherry pie filling	1
1	can (14oz/398mL) crushed pineapple, undrained	1
1	large Cool Whip	1
1	can sweetened condensed milk	1

Mix all the ingredients together, reserving ⅓ cup (75mL) Cool Whip for garnish. Serve in a large bowl or individual stemmed dessert dishes or wine glasses. Garnish with Cool Whip.
This dessert also freezes beautifully. Thaw and stir before serving.
Serves 16.

Meringues

4		egg whites	4	
¼	tsp	cream of tartar	1	mL
1	cup	sugar	250	mL

Preheat oven to 275°F (140°C).
Beat egg whites and cream of tartar until soft peaks form. Add sugar very gradually beating until stiff and glossy. Line a baking sheet with foil and grease. Spread meringue into a 9" (22cm) circle, making sides higher to form a shell.
Bake for 1½ hours. Turn off heat and let cool in oven for 3 hours.

Cottage Pudding

1	lb	low fat cottage cheese	500 g
2		eggs	2
½	cup	sugar	125 mL
½	cup	milk	125 mL
⅓	cup	cream of wheat cereal	75 mL
½	tsp	vanilla	2 mL
		grated peel of 1 large lemon	
½	cup	raisins	125 mL

Preheat oven to 350°F (180°C).
Place the first 7 ingredients in a food processor and blend until smooth. Stir in raisins and pour into a greased 4 cup (1L) baking dish. Place pudding dish in a roasting pan of hot water.
Bake for 1 hour or until knife inserted in centre comes out clean.
Serves 6.

Fresh Citrus Dip

1		egg, slightly beaten	1
¼	cup	fresh orange juice	50 mL
2½	Tbsp	honey	37 mL
¼	tsp	cinnamon	1 mL
		pinch of nutmeg	
1	cup	plain yogurt	250 mL
		sprig of fresh mint for garnish	

Combine the first 5 ingredients in a saucepan. Cook and stir over low heat until thickened. Fold yogurt into cooked mixture. Cover and chill. When ready to serve, place dip in a bowl and garnish with mint. Surround the bowl with a variety of sliced fresh seasonal fruits.
Makes 1½ cups (375mL).

Lemon Pudding Cake

A favourite with the family.

Sauce

1		lemon, juice and grated rind	1
½	cup	sugar	125 mL
1	Tbsp	butter	15 mL
1		egg, beaten	1
1½	cups	boiling water	375 mL

Cake

½	cup	sugar	125 mL
1	Tbsp	butter, softened	15 mL
1		egg, beaten	1
2	Tbsp	milk	30 mL
⅔	cup	flour	150 mL
1	Tbsp	baking powder	15 mL

Preheat oven to 350°F (180°C).
Mix sauce ingredients, in order given, in an 8" (19cm) square pan.
Mix cake ingredients in order and drop by spoonfuls onto the sauce.
Bake for 30 minutes.
Serves 6.

Old-fashioned Lemon Snow

1		envelope unflavoured gelatin	1
¼	cup	cold water	50 mL
1	cup	boiling water	250 mL
⅔	cup	sugar	150 mL
¼	cup	lemon juice	50 mL
1	Tbsp	grated lemon rind	15 mL
2		egg whites, stiffly beaten	2

Soak gelatin in cold water for 5 minutes, then dissolve in boiling water. Add the next 3 ingredients and stir until sugar is dissolved. Chill until syrupy then beat until light and fluffy. Fold in beaten egg whites. Chill until set.
Serves 4.

Custard Sauce

May be served over Old-fashioned Lemon Snow.

2		egg yolks	2
1	cup	milk	250 mL
1-2	tsp	sugar	5-10 mL
½	tsp	vanilla	2 mL

Beat ingredients together and cook in a double boiler over low heat until mixture thickens enough to coat a spoon, but is still thin. Chill. Makes about 1⅓ cups (325mL) sauce.

Coconut Impossible Pie

A company dessert that takes just seconds to prepare.

4		eggs	4
2	cups	2% milk	500 mL
1	cup	sugar	250 mL
1	cup	flaked coconut	250 mL
½	cup	flour	125 mL
¼	cup	melted butter	50 mL
1	tsp	vanilla	5 mL
½	tsp	baking powder	2 mL
¼	tsp	salt	1 mL

Preheat oven to 350°F (180°C).
Combine all the ingredients and beat until smooth. Pour into greased 10" (25cm) pie plate.
Bake for 1 hour. A crust will form on the bottom, custard in the middle and coconut on the top. Best served slightly warm from the oven on the day it is made.
Note: Serve with a pool of raspberry sauce under each slice.
Serves 8.

Raspberry Sauce

2	cups	fresh or frozen raspberries	500 mL
¼	cup	berry sugar	50 mL
¼	cup	brandy (optional)	50 mL

Combine the berries with sugar and let stand at room temperature for at least one hour. Press through a sieve to remove seeds. Add brandy, if desired, and chill until serving time.
Makes about 1 cup (250mL).

Orange Mincemeat Cheesecake

A lovely dessert for your Christmas party.

1	cup	vanilla wafer crumbs	250 mL
¼	cup	melted butter	50 mL
1½	cups	mincemeat	375 mL
4	cups	mini marshmallows	1 L
⅓	cup	fresh orange juice	75 mL
8	oz	cream cheese	250 g
1	Tbsp	grated orange rind	15 mL
1	cup	whipping cream,whipped	250 mL

Preheat oven to 350°F (180°C).
Combine the first 2 ingredients and press into a 9"(22cm) springform pan.
Bake for 10 minutes. Cover with mincemeat. Bake until bubbly, about 15 minutes. Let cool. In top of a double boiler, melt marshmallows with orange juice. Let cool about 20 minutes. Blend cream cheese and orange rind in food processor. Add marshmallow mixture, blending well. Fold in whipped cream. Spread over mincemeat and chill until firm. Garnish with extra mincemeat, whipped cream and holly sprigs.
Note: This dessert freezes well.
Serves 10-12.

Hawaiian Grape Cheesecake

Make a day ahead.

1½	cups	graham wafer crumbs	375 mL
½	cup	sugar	125 mL
⅓	cup	butter, melted	75 mL
1		envelope unflavoured gelatin	1
½	cup	sugar	125 mL
½		can (12½oz/355mL) frozen pink lemonade, defrosted	½
1½	cups	low fat cottage cheese	375 mL
1	tsp	vanilla	5 mL
½	lb	seedless green grapes	250 g
1		can (19oz/540mL) pineapple chunks, well drained	1
1	cup	whipping cream, whipped	250 mL

Combine the first 3 ingredients and press into an 8"(20cm) or a 9"(22cm) spring form pan. To prepare filling, combine the next 3 ingredients in a small saucepan and cook, stirring constantly, until gelatin is dissolved. Cool slightly. Beat cottage cheese until smooth. Stir in gelatin mixture and vanilla. Chill until partially set. Fold in remaining ingredients. Spoon into crust and chill overnight. Garnish with frosted grapes.
Serves 10-12.

Easy Cheesecake

A family favourite that can be made in advance.

Base

1	cup	flour	250 mL
⅔	cup	sugar	150 mL
1	tsp	baking powder	5 mL
½	cup	butter, softened	125 mL
2		eggs, beaten to blend	2
1	Tbsp	milk	15 mL
1	tsp	vanilla	5 mL

Filling

1	cup	cream cheese, softened	250 mL
½	cup	sugar	125 mL
½	cup	sour cream	125 mL
2		eggs, beaten to blend	2
1	tsp	vanilla	5 mL

Preheat oven to 350°F (180°C).
Combine the first 3 ingredients in a mixing bowl. Add the next 4 ingredients and mix well. Spread over bottom and up sides of a greased and floured 10"(25cm) pie plate. Combine cheese and sugar and beat until smooth. Mix in remaining ingredients. Pour over base. Bake for 50 minutes or until edges are browned and centre is springy. Cool completely. Cover with plastic wrap and refrigerate 24 hours or up to 3 days. Serve with a little strawberry sauce poured along one side of each wedge and a few sliced strawberries when in season.

Sauce

1		pkg (10oz/300g) unsweetened strawberries	1
1	Tbsp	icing sugar	15 mL

Combine strawberries and sugar in a blender and process.
Serves 8.

Fruited Eggnog Pie

A rich festive dessert.

1	cup	snipped dried apricots	250	mL
3	Tbsp	rum or orange juice	45	mL
1		envelope unflavoured gelatin	1	
¼	cup	sugar	50	mL
2	cups	commercial eggnog	500	mL
1	cup	whipping cream, whipped	250	mL
1½	tsp	vanilla	7	mL
¼	tsp	almond extract	1	mL
1		baked 9" (22cm) pie shell	1	

Soak apricots in rum and set aside. In a saucepan combine gelatin and sugar. Stir in eggnog. Cook and stir over medium heat until gelatin dissolves, about 5 minutes. Remove from heat and chill until mixture mounds slightly when spooned. Add apricots and remaining ingredients and pile into pie shell. Refrigerate until set.
Note: 1½ cups drained fruit cocktail may be substituted for the apricots and rum.
Serves 8.

Light and Tasty Fruit Pie

1	tsp	butter	5	mL
3	Tbsp	graham cracker crumbs	45	mL
2		cans (10oz/284mL) mandarin orange segments	2	
1		envelope plain gelatin	1	
1	tsp	grated lemon peel	5	mL
1½	cups	each, fresh raspberries and blueberries	375	mL

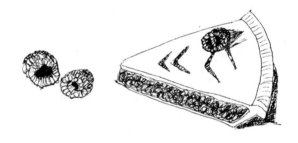

Butter sides and bottom of a 9" (22cm) pie plate. Sprinkle with crumbs and shake to thoroughly coat. Refrigerate 10 minutes to set. Drain liquid from oranges into a saucepan. Sprinkle gelatin over and let stand for 5 minutes. Heat over low heat and stir to dissolve. Stir in lemon peel. Arrange orange slices on bottom of chilled crust, sprinkle raspberries over, then blueberries. Pour gelatin mixture over fruit and refrigerate for 3-4 hours.
Serves 6-8.

Peanut Butter Pie

A decadent confection for peanut butter fans.

Crust

1	cup	chocolate wafer crumbs	250 mL
¼	cup	butter or margarine, melted	50 mL
2	Tbsp	sugar	30 mL

Preheat oven to 350°F (180°C).
Combine ingredients and press into a 9"(22cm) pie plate.
Bake 7 minutes. Cool and chill.

Filling

1		pkg (8oz/250g) cream cheese	1
1	cup	creamy smooth peanut butter (not homemade)	250 mL
¾	cup	icing sugar	175 mL
1	Tbsp	vanilla	15 mL
½	cup	whipping cream, whipped	125 mL

Beat cream cheese and peanut butter until fluffy, beat in sugar and vanilla. Gently fold in whipped cream. Spoon into chilled pie shell. Refrigerate until firm.

Topping

½	cup	whipping cream	125 mL
6	oz	chocolate chips	170 g
¼	cup	chopped unsalted peanuts (optional)	50 mL

Heat whipping cream in a saucepan, add chocolate and stir until melted. Pour over firm pie filling. Sprinkle with nuts. Refrigerate until firm.
Serves 8.

Chunky Chocolate Pecan Pie

Pure decadence.

1		10" (25cm) deep dish pie shell	1
2	cups	pecans	500 mL
6	oz	semisweet chocolate, chopped in ⅜" (1cm) chunks	170 g
3	Tbsp	flour	45 mL
¾	cup	butter	175 mL
¾	cup	brown sugar	175 mL
5		large eggs	5
¾	cup	light corn syrup	175 mL
2	Tbsp	coffee liqueur	30 mL
2	tsp	vanilla	10 mL
1	cup	whipping cream, whipped (optional)	250 mL

Pie Shell
Preheat oven to 375°F (190°C).
Bake pie shell until light golden brown 12-15 minutes. Remove from oven and cool.

Filling
Mix pecans, chocolate and flour in a bowl and set aside. In a large bowl, cream butter and sugar until light and fluffy. Add eggs one at a time, beating well after each addition. Add remaining ingredients (except cream) and beat until smooth. Mix in chocolate nut mixture. Pour into crust.
Reduce oven temperature to 350°F (180°C) and bake for 1 hour or until sides are set.
Serve at room temperature topped with whipped cream if desired.
Serves 10.

Black Forest Roll

Black Forest cake in a roll.

6		egg whites	6	
¼	cup	sugar	50	mL
6		egg yolks	6	
½	cup	sugar	125	mL
1	tsp	vanilla	5	mL
6	Tbsp	flour	90	mL
5	Tbsp	cocoa	75	mL
1½	tsp	baking powder	7	mL
		pinch of salt		
⅔		can (19oz/540mL) cherry pie filling	⅔	
1	cup	whipping cream, whipped	250	mL
1	Tbsp	cocoa	15	mL
2	Tbsp	sugar	30	mL

Preheat oven to 350°F (180°C).
Beat the first 2 ingredients until stiff. Beat together the next 3 ingredients. Gently fold in sifted dry ingredients then add egg whites. Spread batter onto a 10x15" (25x38cm) wax paper-lined cookie sheet.
Bake for 15 minutes only.
Turn out cake onto a tea towel which has been sprinkled with sugar. Carefully remove wax paper. Roll up from narrow edge. Let cool. Unroll and spread with cherry pie filling then a small amount of whipped cream. Roll up carefully and place on serving plate. Add cocoa and sugar to remaining whipped cream, blending well. Ice log. Refrigerate several hours before serving.
Note: This dessert freezes well - freeze first then wrap.
Serves 10-12.

Danish Almond Puff

An unusual puff pastry dessert.

Base

1	cup	flour	250 mL	
½	cup	butter	125 mL	
2	Tbsp	cold water	30 mL	

Middle Layer

1	cup	water	250 mL	
½	cup	butter	125 mL	
1	tsp	almond extract	5 mL	
1	cup	flour	250 mL	
3		eggs	3	

Frosting

1¾	cups	icing sugar	425 mL	
¼	cup	butter	50 mL	
1		egg white	1	
½	tsp	vanilla	2 mL	
¼	tsp	almond extract	1 mL	

Preheat oven to 350°F (180°C).
Cut butter into flour as for a pie crust. Sprinkle water over and mix with a fork to moisten. Press dough onto an ungreased cookie sheet in two 3x12" (7.5x30cm) rectangular strips. Set aside. Put water and butter in a saucepan and heat to boiling. Add almond extract and remove from heat. Add flour all at once and mix vigorously until mixture forms a ball. Add eggs, one at a time, beating well after each. Spread this mixture evenly over the strips.
Bake for 1 hour. Frost while warm.

Frosting

Cream butter in a small bowl. Add sugar alternately with egg white beating until light and fluffy. Stir in extracts.
Serves 8-10.

Cookies and Squares

Five Star Cookies

Loaded with good chewy flavour.

2	cups	flour	500 mL
1	tsp	soda	5 mL
1	lb	dates, cut up	500 g
1½	cups	brown sugar	375 mL
1	cup	butter or margarine	250 mL
2		eggs	2
1	tsp	vanilla	5 mL
1	cup	rolled oats	250 mL
½	cup	shredded coconut	125 mL
½	cup	chopped walnuts	125 mL

Preheat oven to 375°F (190°C).
Sift flour and soda over dates. Cream sugar and butter, beat in eggs and vanilla. Add remaining ingredients mixing thoroughly. Drop by spoonfuls onto a lightly greased cookie sheet.
Bake for 8-10 minutes.
Makes 7-8 dozen.

Chocolate Chunk Cookies

The ultimate cookie.

½	cup	butter, softened	125 mL
½	cup	white sugar	125 mL
¼	cup	brown sugar	50 mL
1		egg, beaten	1
1	tsp	vanilla	5 mL
1¼	cups	flour	300 mL
2	tsp	cocoa	10 mL
½	tsp	baking soda	2 mL
6	oz	semi-sweet chocolate, chopped	170 g
½	cup	chopped walnuts	125 mL

Preheat oven to 325°F (160°C).
Cream butter and sugar, beat in egg and vanilla. Combine flour, cocoa and baking soda and mix into butter mixture. Stir in chocolate and nuts. Form into large walnut size balls and place on a lightly greased cookie sheet.
Bake for 20 minutes.
Makes 24 large cookies.

Date Oat Bran Cookies

Quick, good-tasting and super for the lunchbox.

1	cup	brown sugar	250 mL
½	cup	margarine	125 mL
1		egg	1
2	tsp	vanilla	10 mL
1¼	cups	whole wheat flour	300 mL
1	cup	oat bran	250 mL
1	tsp	soda	5 mL
1	tsp	baking powder	5 mL
1	cup	chopped dates	250 mL
½	cup	chopped walnuts	125 mL

Preheat oven to 350°F (180°C).
In a large bowl, cream together the first 4 ingredients. Combine the dry ingredients and stir into creamed mixture. Mix in dates and nuts. Drop by tablespoonfuls onto lightly greased cookie sheet.
Bake for 15 minutes or until golden.
Makes 3 dozen cookies.

Granola Cookies

Chewy good cookies.

1	cup	butter or margarine	250 mL
¾	cup	brown sugar	175 mL
½	cup	white sugar	125 mL
2		eggs	2
2	Tbsp	grated orange rind	30 mL
1	tsp	vanilla	5 mL
3	cups	granola	750 mL
1¾	cups	flour	425 mL
1	tsp	soda	5 mL
1	tsp	ginger	5 mL

Preheat oven to 375°F (190°C).
Cream butter and sugar, beat in eggs, rind and vanilla. Combine the remaining ingredients and add to first mixture, mixing well. Drop by spoonfuls onto greased baking sheets.
Bake for 12-15 minutes.
Note: Granola recipe page 190.
Makes 4 dozen large cookies.

Favourite Ginger Cookies

2	cups	brown sugar	500 mL
1½	cups	shortening, softened	375 mL
¾	cup	molasses	175 mL
2		eggs	2
4½	cups	flour	1 L
4	tsp	soda	20 mL
2	tsp	cinnamon	10 mL
2	tsp	ginger	10 mL
1	tsp	ground cloves	5 mL
⅓	cup	sugar	75 mL

Preheat oven to 350°F (180°C).
In a large bowl cream together the first 4 ingredients. Combine the next 5 ingredients and add to creamed mixture. Form into walnut size balls, roll in sugar and place on lightly greased cookie sheet. Do not crowd as cookies spread.
Bake for 10-12 minutes.
Makes 7 dozen cookies.

Orange Oatmeal Cookies

1	cup	butter or margarine	250 mL
2	cups	brown sugar	500 mL
2		eggs	2
3	Tbsp	orange juice	45 mL
2	Tbsp	grated orange rind	30 mL
2	cups	flour	500 mL
1	tsp	baking powder	5 mL
¾	tsp	salt	3 mL
2	cups	rolled oats	500 mL
1	cup	raisins	250 mL
½	cup	chopped nuts	125 mL

Preheat oven to 350°F (180°C).
Cream butter and sugar until light. Beat in eggs, juice and rind.
Combine the next 3 ingredients and stir into creamed mixture. Add
remaining ingredients and mix thoroughly. Drop by tablespoonfuls
onto greased cookie sheet.
Bake for 10-12 minutes.
Makes 36 large cookies.

Date Chip Squares

It's so-o-o delicious.

1½	cups	chopped dates	375	mL
1½	cups	boiling water	375	mL
1	tsp	baking soda	5	mL
¾	cup	butter	175	mL
1	cup	sugar	250	mL
2		eggs	2	
2	cups	flour	500	mL
1	Tbsp	cocoa	15	mL
1	tsp	baking powder	5	mL

Topping

½	cup	brown sugar	125	mL
2	Tbsp	butter, softened	30	mL
¾	cup	chopped nuts	175	mL
½	cup	chocolate chips	125	mL

Preheat oven to 350°F (180°C).
Place dates in a bowl, sprinkle with soda and pour boiling water over. Set aside to cool. Cream butter and sugar, add eggs and vanilla. Stir in date mixture, blending well. Sift dry ingredients and stir into batter. Spread evenly into a greased and floured 9x13" (22x34cm) pan. Mix together topping ingredients and sprinkle over batter.
Bake for 45 minutes.
Makes 24 large squares.

Square Chocolate Chippers

These cookies can be mixed and in the oven in 5 minutes and are "oh so good".

1	cup	butter or margarine, softened	250 mL
1	cup	brown sugar	250 mL
2	cups	flour	500 mL
1	cup	chocolate chips	250 mL
1	cup	chopped walnuts	250 mL

Preheat oven to 350°F (180°C).
Cream butter and sugar. Mix in flour, then chips and nuts. Pat into a 10x15" (25x38cm) pan.
Bake for 25 minutes or until golden. Cut in squares while still warm.
Makes 36 large cookies.

Chocolate Tornadoes

Bake these moist double chocolate brownies in a round pan and cut in wedges to serve.

1	cup	sugar	250 mL
½	cup	butter or margarine	125 mL
2		eggs, beaten	2
1	tsp	vanilla	5 mL
½	cup	flour	125 mL
⅓	cup	cocoa	75 mL
½	cup	chopped almonds, toasted	125 mL
½	cup	chocolate chips	125 mL

Preheat oven to 350°F (180°C).
Cream sugar and butter, beat in eggs and vanilla. Mix in flour and cocoa, then nuts and chocolate. Spread into a greased 9" (22cm) pie plate or spring form pan.
Bake for 30 minutes.
Note: Serve for dessert with a little raspberry sauce (page 159) spooned down one side of each wedge.
Makes 12 wedges.

Apricot Bars

1½	cups	flour	375 mL
1½	cups	quick oats	375 mL
1	cup	brown sugar	250 mL
1	tsp	baking powder	5 mL
¾	cup	melted butter or margarine	175 mL
2	cups	apricot jam	500 mL

Preheat oven to 350°F (180°C).
Stir together the first 4 ingredients. Add butter and mix. Press ⅔
into a greased 9x13" (22x34cm) pan. Dot jam over top, gently spread
to level. Sprinkle with remaining crumbs and pat down slightly.
Bake for 30 minutes.
Makes 2½-3 dozen bars.

Pink Slice

2	cups	crushed graham wafers, about 25	500 mL
½	cup	medium coconut	125 mL
½	cup	chopped glace cherries	125 mL
½	cup	brown sugar	125 mL
½	cup	butter	125 mL
1		egg, well beaten	1

Combine the first 3 ingredients and set aside. In a saucepan,
combine the remaining ingredients. Bring to a boil over medium
heat, stirring constantly, and boil gently for 1 minute. Remove from
heat. Stir in graham wafer mixture, blending well. Press into an
8"(19cm) square pan. Ice while still warm with butter icing coloured
with maraschino cherry juice or red food colouring. Refer to *Fast and
Fantastic*, page 170. Refrigerate, then cut into squares.
Note: Boxed graham wafer crumbs are too fine for this recipe.
Makes 20-25 squares.

Swedish Almond Cake

1		egg, beaten	1
½	cup	sugar	125 mL
½	cup	butter or margarine	125 mL
1	cup	flour	250 mL
1	tsp	almond extract	5 mL
⅓	cup	flaked almonds	75 mL

Preheat oven to 375°F (190°C).
In a mixing bowl beat the first 5 ingredients in the order given.
Spread in an 8" (19cm) square pan. Sprinkle with almonds.
Bake for 20-30 minutes or until golden.
Makes 16 squares.

Pender Harbour Bars

3	cups	rolled oats	750 mL
1	cup	chocolate chips	250 mL
½	cup	coconut	125 mL
½	cup	sunflower seeds	125 mL
½	cup	raisins, dates or combination	125 mL
⅓	cup	wheat germ	75 mL
¼	cup	slivered almonds (optional)	50 mL
2	Tbsp	sesame seeds	30 mL
¾	cup	brown sugar	175 mL
⅔	cup	peanut butter	150 mL
½	cup	corn syrup	125 mL
½	cup	melted butter	125 mL
2	Tbsp	vanilla	30 mL

Preheat oven to 350°F (180°C).
In a large bowl combine the first 8 ingredients. Combine the next 5
ingredients and mix thoroughly into the first mixture. Press into a
9x13"(22x34cm) pan.
Bake for 15-20 minutes.
Makes 24 large bars.

Butter Tart Slice

Butter tarts in a square. Even more delicious the next day.

1½	cups	flour	375 mL
½	cup	butter	125 mL
2	Tbsp	icing sugar	30 mL
2		eggs, well beaten	2
1½	cups	brown sugar	375 mL
¼	cup	melted butter	50 mL
1	Tbsp	vinegar	15 mL
1	tsp	vanilla	5 mL
1	cup	raisins	250 mL
½	cup	chopped walnuts (optional)	125 mL

Preheat oven to 350°F (180°C).
For the base combine the first 3 ingredients with a pastry blender.
Press into an oiled 9" (22cm) square pan.
Bake for 10 minutes. Combine the remaining ingredients, mixing well. Pour over base.
Bake for 30-40 minutes. Check frequently to avoid burning.
Note: This recipe can be doubled using a 9x13"(22x34cm) pan.
Makes 25 squares or more.

Peanut Butter Nanaimo Bars

A new twist for an old favourite.

½	cup	sugar	125 mL
½	cup	corn syrup	125 mL
1	cup	peanut butter	250 mL
3	cups	Rice Krispies	750 mL
¼	cup	flaked coconut	50 mL
2	cups	sifted icing sugar	500 mL
¼	cup	butter, softened	50 mL
3	Tbsp	milk	45 mL
2	Tbsp	vanilla custard powder	30 mL
1	cup	chocolate chips	250 mL

Combine sugar and corn syrup in a heavy saucepan. Cook and stir until sugar dissolves. Stir in peanut butter. Remove from heat and mix in Rice Krispies and coconut. Press into a 9" (22cm) square pan. Cool.

Cream the next 4 ingredients and spread over base. Chill until set. Melt chocolate, cool slightly and spread over top. Before chocolate sets, mark into squares by cutting through chocolate. This prevents the chocolate top from cracking.

Makes 16-20 squares.

Cappuccino Bars

2	tsp	instant coffee	10 mL
1	tsp	vanilla	5 mL
½	tsp	water	2 mL
2	cups	flour	500 mL
1	tsp	cinnamon	5 mL
1	cup	butter or margarine, softened	250 mL
½	cup	white sugar	125 mL
½	cup	brown sugar	125 mL
1		egg yolk	1
1	cup	chocolate chips	250 mL
1	cup	chopped walnuts or pecans	250 mL

Preheat oven to 350°F (180°C).
Stir coffee, vanilla and water together until coffee dissolves. Set aside. Stir flour and cinnamon together and set aside. Beat butter and sugar until fluffy. Mix in egg yolk and coffee mixture. Gradually add flour mixture, beating until combined. Press into a 9x13" (22x34cm) pan.
Bake for 15-18 minutes.
Remove from the oven and immediately sprinkle with chocolate chips. Let stand until melted. Spread evenly and sprinkle with nuts.
Makes 48 small bars.

Capilano Chocolate Bars

1	cup	flour	250 mL
½	cup	butter	125 mL
¼	cup	sugar	50 mL
¼	cup	cocoa	50 mL
1	cup	raisins	250 mL
2		eggs, well beaten	2
1	cup	brown sugar	250 mL
1	tsp	flour	5 mL
1	tsp	baking powder	5 mL
1	tsp	vanilla	5 mL

Preheat oven to 350°F (180°C).
Using a pastry cutter, blend together the first 4 ingredients until crumbly. Press into an ungreased 9x9" (22x22cm) pan.
Bake for 12-15 minutes.
In a small bowl pour boiling water over raisins to plump them up. Drain them and set aside. Beat together the remaining ingredients. Stir in raisins and pour the mixture over the base.
Bake for 20-25 minutes. Cool before icing.

Icing

1	cup	icing sugar	250 mL
¼	cup	cocoa	50 mL
3	Tbsp	butter, softened	45 mL
1	Tbsp	hot coffee	15 mL

Combine ingredients and beat until smooth. If icing is too thick add a little more coffee. Spread over cooled bars.
Makes 25 squares.

Fudge Krispies

1		pkg (12oz/350g) chocolate chips	1
½	cup	margarine	125 mL
½	cup	corn syrup	125 mL
⅓	cup	icing sugar	75 mL
1	tsp	vanilla	5 mL
6	cups	crisp rice cereal	1.5 L

Melt together the first 3 ingredients over low heat. Stir in the sugar and vanilla. Add the crisp rice cereal, mixing well. Spread into a greased 9x13" (22x34cm) pan.
Chill and cut in squares.
Makes 36 squares.

Snappy Pecan Bars

2	Tbsp	margarine, melted	30 mL
1	cup	brown sugar	250 mL
1		egg	1
1	cup	flour	250 mL
1	tsp	baking powder	5 mL
¾	cup	coarsely chopped pecans	175 mL

Preheat oven to 300°F (150°C).
Stir melted margarine into sugar. Beat in egg then mix in the remaining ingredients. Spread into a greased 8" (19cm) square pan. Bake for 40 minutes. Cut into squares while hot.
Makes 24 bars.

Etcetera

Garden Delight Pickles

3	lb	silverskin onions, blanched to remove skins	1.5 kg
1½	lb	whole dill cukes, cut in bite size chunks	750 g
1½		cauliflowers, cut in bite size chunks	1½
3		green peppers, chopped	3
1		red pepper, chopped	1
4	qt	ice cold water	4 L
2	cups	pickling salt	500 mL

Sauce

1	cup	flour	250 mL
6	Tbsp	dry mustard	90 mL
1	Tbsp	tumeric	15 mL
8	cups	white vinegar, divided	2 L
2	cups	sugar	500 mL

Soak chopped vegetables in brine overnight. Rinse vegetables using lots of water and drain well.
To prepare sauce, mix the first 3 ingredients with 1½ cups (375mL) vinegar to make a smooth paste. Add remaining vinegar and sugar. Heat gently to boiling, stirring constantly with a flat whisk. Do not burn. When bubbling and thickened, add vegetables. Heat thoroughly but don't cook vegetables until soft. Immediately fill hot sterilized jars and seal with hot sterilized lids.
Makes 10-11 pints.

Red Tomato Chutney

2	lb	ripe tomatoes, peeled and chopped	1	kg
6		onions, chopped	6	
2		apples, peeled and chopped	2	
2		carrots, grated or chopped	2	
1	lb	brown sugar	500	g
1	cup	malt vinegar	250	mL
1	Tbsp	salt	15	mL
1	Tbsp	dry mustard	15	mL
1	Tbsp	curry powder	15	mL
2	Tbsp	cornstarch	30	mL
3	Tbsp	vinegar	45	mL

Combine the first 9 ingredients and simmer for 1¼ hours. Combine cornstarch and vinegar. Stir into chutney cooking until thickened, about 5 minutes. Pour into hot sterilized jars.
Makes approximately 3 jars.

Garam Masala

This is one of many versions of garam masala. Add it to a dish just before serving.

1½	Tbsp	ground coriander	22	mL
1½	Tbsp	ground cumin	22	mL
1	Tbsp	ground cardamom	15	mL
1	Tbsp	ground ginger	15	mL
1	Tbsp	ground cinnamon	15	mL
2	tsp	curry powder	10	mL
2	tsp	nutmeg	10	mL
1	tsp	ground pepper	5	mL
1	tsp	mace	5	mL

Combine ingredients and store in tightly covered jar.
Makes ½ cup (125mL).

Microwave Peanut Brittle

1	cup	white sugar	250 mL
½	cup	white corn syrup	125 mL
1	cup	salted roasted peanuts	250 mL
1	tsp	margarine	5 mL
1	tsp	vanilla	5 mL
1	tsp	baking soda	5 mL

Combine the sugar and corn syrup in a 4 cup (1L) measuring cup and microwave at high for 5 minutes. Add nuts, stir, and microwave another 4 minutes. Add margarine and vanilla and microwave 2 minutes. Add soda and stir until foamy. Spread onto a buttered cookie sheet. Cool and break into pieces.
Makes about 1 lb (500g).

Nutty Popcorn

A treat for the family and wonderful as gifts.

2¾	cups	brown sugar	675 mL
1½	cups	butter	375 mL
1	cup	white corn syrup	250 mL
1	tsp	vanilla	5 mL
24	cups	popped popcorn	5-6 L
3	cups	assorted nuts	750 mL
		eg peanuts, pecans, slivered almonds, hazelnuts, *etc*	

Preheat oven to 250°F (120°C).
Bring the first 3 ingredients to a boil in a saucepan. Stir to dissolve sugar. Remove from heat and stir in vanilla. Pour over combined popcorn and nuts, stirring to coat evenly. Place in 2 or 3 large roasting pans or sided cookie sheets.
Bake for 1¼ hours, stirring thoroughly every 20 minutes.
Makes 6 quarts (6L).

Hot Spiced Punch

The spices fill the house with a wonderful aroma.

10	cups	pineapple juice	2.5 L
8	cups	cranberry juice	2 L
7	cups	water	1.75 L
1	cup	brown sugar	250 mL
4	Tbsp	whole cloves	60 mL
4	Tbsp	whole allspice	60 mL
12		sticks cinnamon,broken	12
1	tsp	salt (optional)	5 mL

Pour juices and water into a 30 or 40 cup coffee percolator. Place remaining ingredients in the percolator basket. Perk through cycle. Note: Also good spiked with rum.
Serves 30.

Kool Punch

Don't be put off by the Kool-Aid - it's delicious.

1		can (12½oz/355mL) frozen orange juice	1
½	cup	sugar	125 mL
⅓	cup	freshly squeezed lemon juice	75 mL
1		envelope unsweetened Kool-Aid (cherry or raspberry flavour)	1
1		bottle (2qt/2L) club soda	1

Place the first 4 ingredients in an ice-cream pail and mix together. Add water to two-thirds full. Freeze overnight. Remove from freezer 5-6 hours before serving. Place in punch bowl and add club soda. Garnish with orange slices.
Serves 15.

Super Granola

Super good! Super nutritious!

5	cups	rolled oats	1.25	L
1	cup	triticale or barley flakes	250	mL
1	cup	whole wheat flour	250	mL
1	cup	skim milk powder	250	mL
1	cup	natural bran	250	mL
1	cup	coconut	250	mL
1	cup	slivered almonds	250	mL
1	cup	raw cashew pieces	250	mL
1	cup	raw sunflower seeds	250	mL
1	cup	raw pumpkin seeds	250	mL
½	cup	raw sesame seeds	125	mL
½	cup	wheat germ	125	mL
1	cup	water	250	mL
¾	cup	liquid honey	175	mL
½	cup	vegetable oil	125	mL

Preheat oven to 275°F (140°C).
Combine the first 12 ingredients in a very large bowl. Heat the remaining ingredients together, stirring to combine. Pour over first mixture and blend thoroughly. Spread on 2 large cookie sheets with sides or shallow roasting pans.
Bake for 1 hour or until golden, stirring several times.
Note: Dried fruit, *eg* raisins, apricots, bananas, peaches, *etc* may be added after baking.
Makes 16 cups.

White Sauce Mix

Wonderful to have in the refrigerator for a last minute sauce.

2½	cups	powdered skim milk	625 mL
1	cup	butter or margarine	250 mL
1½	cups	flour	375 mL
2	tsp	salt	10 mL
½	tsp	ground white pepper	2 mL

Blend ingredients until the consistency of sand. For 1 cup (250mL) sauce, use ½ cup (125mL) mix to 1 cup (250mL) water and cook, stirring until smooth.

Dijon Mustard

2	cups	dry white wine	500 mL
1	cup	chopped onion	250 mL
3		cloves garlic, minced	3
½	cup	dry mustard	125 mL
2	Tbsp	honey	30 mL
1	Tbsp	vegetable oil	15 mL
2	tsp	salt	10 mL
		few drops Tabasco sauce	

Combine the first 3 ingredients in a saucepan and heat to boiling. Lower heat and simmer 5 minutes. Strain into dry mustard, beating until very smooth. Add remaining ingredients. Return to pan and heat slowly, stirring constantly until mixture thickens. Cool. Pour into a hot sterilized jar and refrigerate at least 3 days before using. Makes approximately 2 cups (500mL).

90's Crème Fraîche

A light version of this popular topping.

½	cup	whole milk yogurt	125 mL
½	cup	homogenized milk	125 mL

Drain yogurt in a coffee filter for 45 minutes. Combine with milk. Cover tightly and keep at room temperature for 24 hours. Refrigerate up to 2 weeks.
Makes 1 cup.

French Pistou

This French version of pesto sauce comes from Kerry Moore, Food and Environment writer for the Province newspaper.

5		cloves garlic, chopped	5
½	cup	chopped fresh basil or 5 Tbsp (75mL) dried	125 mL
2	Tbsp	tomato paste	30 mL
½	cup	freshly grated Parmesan cheese	125 mL
6	Tbsp	olive oil	90 mL

In a blender or food processor mix the garlic and basil into a paste. Add the remaining ingredients and process until blended.
Note: Traditionally used to flavour soupe au pistou. Try a little mixed with mayonnaise for sandwiches.
Makes about ¾ cup (175mL).

Index

MORE FAST AND FANTASTIC
North Shore Family Services Society
#303-126 East 15th Street
North Vancouver BC   V7L 2P9
Fax (604) 988 3961

Please send me _____ copies of **MORE FAST AND FANTASTIC** at $12.95 per copy (plus $3.00 per copy for postage and handling). Or send me one copy each of **FAST AND FANTASTIC** and **MORE FAST AND FANTASTIC** for a limited introductory price of $19.95 for the two volumes. Please send me _____ 2-volume sets at $19.95 (plus $4.50 postage and handling). Enclosed is $_____.
Make cheques or money orders payable to **North Shore Family Services Society.**

NAME

ADDRESS

CITY   PROVINCE   POSTAL CODE

MORE FAST AND FANTASTIC
North Shore Family Services Society
#303-126 East 15th Street
North Vancouver BC   V7L 2P9
Fax (604) 988 3961

Please send me _____ copies of **MORE FAST AND FANTASTIC** at $12.95 per copy (plus $3.00 per copy for postage and handling). Or send me one copy each of **FAST AND FANTASTIC** and **MORE FAST AND FANTASTIC** for a limited introductory price of $19.95 for the two volumes. Please send me _____ 2-volume sets at $19.95 (plus $4.50 postage and handling). Enclosed is $_____.
Make cheques or money orders payable to **North Shore Family Services Society.**

NAME

ADDRESS

CITY   PROVINCE   POSTAL CODE